AMERICAN HERITAGE

THE MAGAZINE OF HISTORY

February, 1977 · Volume XXVIII · Number 2

EDITOR
Alvin M. Josephy, Jr.

MANAGING EDITOR Nat Brandt
ART DIRECTOR Emma Landau
BOARD OF EDITORS
E. M. Halliday, *Chairman*
Bruce Catton, Barbara Klaw,
Richard F. Snow, Geoffrey C. Ward, T. H. Watkins
PICTURE EDITORS
Devorah K. Cohen, Carla Davidson, Mary Dawn Earley
COPY EDITOR Brenda Savard
EDITORIAL ASSISTANTS
Elizabeth Oettinger, Mary Elizabeth Wise
CONTRIBUTING EDITORS
Robert C. Alberts, Allan L. Damon,
Joan Paterson Kerr, Bernard A. Weisberger
ADVISORY BOARD
Henry Steele Commager,
Marshall B. Davidson, John A. Garraty,
Eugene D. Genovese, William H. Goetzmann,
Archibald Hanna, Louis C. Jones,
Howard H. Peckham, Arthur M. Schlesinger, Jr.

CHIEF, EUROPEAN BUREAU Gertrudis Feliu
LONDON OFFICE Rosemary L. Klein

AMERICAN HERITAGE PUBLISHING COMPANY

CHAIRMAN OF THE BOARD
Samuel P. Reed
PRESIDENT AND PUBLISHER
Rhett Austell
EDITOR IN CHIEF—MAGAZINES
Alvin M. Josephy, Jr.
SENIOR EDITORS
Joseph J. Thorndike, Jr., Oliver Jensen
CONSULTING EDITOR
J. H. Plumb
EDITORIAL ART DIRECTOR Murray Belsky
TREASURER Anthony J. Sansiveri
PROMOTION DIRECTOR Ernest Quick
PROMOTION ART DIRECTOR David Van Inwegen
CIRCULATION AND SALES DIRECTOR Donald B. Barrows, Jr.
PRODUCTION DIRECTOR Elbert Burr

AMERICAN HERITAGE is published every two months by American Heritage Publishing Co., Inc.; editorial and executive offices, 10 Rockefeller Plaza, N.Y., N.Y. 10020. Secretary and Treasurer, Anthony J. Sansiveri. Correspondence about subscriptions should go to American Heritage Subscription Office, 383 West Center St., Marion, Ohio 43302. Single copies: $6. Annual subscriptions: $24 in U.S. and Canada; $26 elsewhere. A 10-year Index of Vols. VI–XV is available at $7.50; 5-year Index of Vols. XVI–XX at $7.50; 5-year Index of Vols. XXI–XXV at $7.50.

AMERICAN HERITAGE considers but assumes no responsibility for unsolicited materials; these require return postage. Title registered U.S. Patent Office. Second-class postage paid at New York, N.Y., and at additional mailing offices.

AMERICAN HERITAGE has been selected by the Library of Congress for reproduction on recordings called Talking Books, distributed free by regional libraries in the U.S. to those unable to use conventional print because of a visual or physical handicap. For information write the Library of Congress, Division for the Blind and Physically Handicapped, 1291 Taylor St., N.W., Washington, D.C. 20542.

Built in an age in which a skyscraper was a celebration of man's ingenuity, not a comment on his anonymity, the great Woolworth Building of 1913 dominated the skyline of Manhattan with a splendid, intricate grace. For the story of "The World's Tallest Building," turn to page 86.
NEW-YORK HISTORICAL SOCIETY

AMERICAN HERITAGE

THE MAGAZINE OF HISTORY

Sponsored by   American Association for State & Local History · Society of American Historians

---

CONTENTS February, 1977 · Volume XXVIII · Number 2

COVER: He stood for the status quo, and for eight years as Speaker (1903–1911) he ruled the House of Representatives in tyrannical fashion, opposed to reform and abusive of critics whether Democrat or Republican. He was the irascible, uncouth, yet somehow lovable Joseph Gurney Cannon—"Uncle Joe"— one of a handful of men who came to symbolize the awesome legislative powers of the Speaker. For who these men were and how they did it, turn to page 26.
LIBRARY OF CONGRESS

by Tom Braden

THE BIRTH OF THE

CIA

The history of successful ideas is sometimes marked by a trade-off. In his old age General William J. Donovan, founder of the United States intelligence service, may have reflected on the phenomenon. The trade-off goes something like this:

A man has an idea and proceeds to push it. Naturally, his idea is opposed by those to whom its acceptance will mean loss of power, stability, and comfort. Often the man is termed "power-mad"; he may even be hated. But suppose the idea is a very good one. There comes a point in the battle when to those who must decide the issue, a compromise occurs. Why not accept the idea and bar the man who had it from having anything to do with carrying it out?

Some such trade-off—trade-offs are never explicitly stated—hit Donovan very hard on a day in January, 1953, when Allen W. Dulles became Director of the Central Intelligence Agency, an institution that had sprung largely out of Donovan's brain.

"Ah," the old soldier sighed when he heard the news, "a very good man, Allen. I chose him personally to be chief of OSS in Switzerland. But Allen is young and inexperienced. He's never had a large command. He ought to be number two."

The emissary from Dulles to whom Donovan made this observation was amused at hearing the sixty-year-old Dulles called "young and inexperienced." But when Donovan's remark was reported back to Dulles, he was understanding. "Poor Bill. He's never wanted anything so much in his life. And you know, if they'd bought Bill's idea in the first place, we'd be a lot better off than we are now."

Dulles was trying to be generous, but he was not exaggerating. Anyone who looks at the early history of the United States intelligence effort must be struck by the time wasted between Donovan and Dulles, or, to put it more precisely, between 1945, when Joseph Stalin opened his cold-war offensive in Poland, and 1950, when the Soviet Union attacked through its satellite in Korea.

During that period Russia erected its iron curtain; threatened Turkey, the Balkans, West Germany, and the Middle East; fought proposals for a United Nations army, international control of atomic energy, and the Marshall Plan; and began its enormously effective hate-America campaign in western Europe. While all this was going on, what might have been a United States counterforce languished in the hands of ineffectual men, subalterns to chieftains who

When and how it got the green light

were carving out empires in a battle over the unification of the armed services.

It was a time when a huge defense establishment was being dismantled at a rate as alarming to the country's leaders as it was popular with the country's people, and when Americans, tired of war and trusting in peace, wanted very much to believe that the leaders of the Soviet Union felt the same way. "Wild Bill" Donovan, with his talk of spies and saboteurs, seemed an anachronism.

The name "Wild Bill" was a generational heritage—a pitcher for the Detroit Tigers named William Donovan walked six and hit one in the first three innings of the deciding game of the World Series of 1909. But it was not an inaccurate sobriquet. Donovan was a fearless soldier and a first-rate lawyer. He had a bland manner, enormous round blue eyes, and a habit of walking on the balls of his feet, like a halfback who might suddenly swerve.

But he was also a romantic, and like all romantics he could be from time to time both endearing and irritating. For example, driving across town in New York City shortly after V-J Day, Donovan suddenly ordered his chauffeur to halt, darted from the car and disappeared into the crowd. Reappearing a few moments later, with a boyish grin, he explained to a companion, "I just remembered I ought to pay my respects to Father Duffy. Haven't talked to him for a long while."

Father Duffy had been regimental chaplain of Donovan's Fighting 69th during World War I and had been on the field when Donovan won the Congressional Medal of Honor. But he had, at this time, been dead for many years. Only a man of endearing romanticism would have thought to confer with his statue in Times Square.

On the other hand, Donovan's romanticism led him to deeds which seemed arrogant. He had himself transported to World War II beaches during landings for no other reason than that he wanted to be there; he went over other peoples' heads; he ignored channels and organization charts. And he would try anything. The more insane the idea, the more likely it seemed that Donovan would wave his hand and say, "Let's give it a try."

To the Army's intelligence branch, G-2, to the Office of Naval Intelligence, to J. Edgar Hoover's FBI, Donovan was anathema. The bureaucracies of these organizations could not abide the thought that this freewheeling, inde-pendent, little round man who had built the Office of Strategic Services, the enormous wartime spy agency, who reported directly to his friend Franklin D. Roosevelt, and whom, throughout the war, the bureaucrats had unsuccessfully endeavored to confine would survive to threaten their responsibilities and prerogatives now that peace had returned and things were going to get back to normal. "A mad man," was the way Major General George V. Strong, chief of the Army's G-2, referred to Donovan privately. Undersecretary of State Dean Acheson expressed the general view: "Donovan would have surprised no one if . . . he left one morning and returned the previous afternoon."

The bureaucracy succeeded in stopping Donovan and in killing his beloved OSS. But history played Donovan's enemies an enormous trick. The intelligence service they created to replace OSS eventually became the Central Intelligence Agency; CIA eventually became almost as powerful as Donovan had envisioned that his OSS in peacetime would be; finally, when Allen Dulles was named Director of CIA, American secret intelligence once again had at its helm a man who had learned his trade in the OSS and would not be long in reverting to the lessons he had learned.

Was it a good thing or a bad thing that Donovan's enemies won their battle and lost their war? The question is still being argued. Is it a good thing or a bad thing that the United States owns a huge secret intelligence agency with a powerful subversive arm? It is not my intent to argue but only to set down what happened. The story begins with the defeat of Donovan.

At five o'clock on the morning of February 9, 1945, the 62-year-old Donovan picked up a copy of the Washington *Times-Herald* on his Georgetown doorstep. There on the front page was his name in headlines and under that the by-line, Walter J. Trohan. The story must have burst upon Donovan like one of those artillery barrages Father Duffy had described after the second Battle of the Marne: "No crescendo about it; just a sudden crash, like an avalanche."

"Creation of an all powerful intelligence service to spy on the postwar world and to pry into the lives of citizens at home is under consideration by the New Deal," it began. "*The Washington Times-Herald* and the *Chicago Tribune* yesterday secured exclusively a copy of a highly confidential

to conduct "subversive operations abroad"

and secret memorandum from General [William J.] Donovan to President Roosevelt . . . also obtained was a copy of an equally secret suggested draft of an order setting up the general intelligence service, which would supersede all existing Federal police and intelligence units, including Army G-2, Navy ONI, the Federal Bureau of Investigation, the Internal Revenue Agency. . . ."

Trohan went on to imply that the new unit would undermine J. Edgar Hoover. It would have secret funds for spy work "along the lines of bribery and luxury living described in the novels of E. Phillips Oppenheim. . . ."

The article, in short, was more than a leak. It was a hatchet job. Donovan finished reading it and called his executive officer, Colonel Ole Doering. Doering still remembers the soft voice on the telephone: "Ole, I want you to find out who did this and report to me at nine."

Doering dressed hurriedly and set about tracing the distribution of the five typed copies of Donovan's plan for peacetime intelligence. "At 9, I was ready," he recalls. "I told the General that J. Edgar Hoover had personally handed the memorandum to Trohan. Donovan never said a word."

Roosevelt did say a word. The President called that afternoon to say that he wanted the whole thing shoved under the rug for as long as the shock waves reverberated. Seven weeks later, Roosevelt judged that the heat was off and released a letter to Donovan giving the plan his general approval and asking Donovan to get comments from members of the Cabinet and other government officials. It was too late. A week later, Roosevelt was dead.

It is important to note the outlines of Donovan's plan for a peacetime intelligence agency because it was the starting point from which the country departed and to which it eventually returned. The chief features were as follows:

First, the director of the new agency would report only to the President. Meaning: power.

Second, the new agency would "collect" intelligence. Meaning: it would have its own sources of information, including spies.

Third, the agency's director would make "final evaluations of intelligence within the government," final "synthesis," and final "dissemination." Meaning: Army and Navy Intelligence and the State Department could continue to perform the work "required by such agencies in the actual performance of their functions and duties," but there would be no doubt as to who was to be boss.

Fourth, the new agency was to have "an independent budget." Meaning: again, power.

Fifth, the agency was to have "no police or law enforcement functions, either at home or abroad." Meaning: Donovan intended no such threat to J. Edgar Hoover as the newspaper revelation implied.

Sixth, the new peacetime agency would conduct "sub-

General William J. ("Wild Bill") Donovan, head of the CIA's prototype, the fabled OSS, after a conference with F.D.R. in 1945

versive operations abroad." Meaning: just that.

In summary, it was to be the wartime OSS taken from under the jealous eye of the Joint Chiefs of Staff, and given the independent power to issue orders to G-2, ONI, the intelligence branch of the Department of State—and to the extent to which J. Edgar Hoover was collecting foreign intelligence in South America, to the FBI.

Trohan had not been far wrong in calling it "all-powerful," though there was no basis in Donovan's memorandum for the suggestion that it would conduct espionage at home, supersede the FBI, or enable its employees to live luxuriously.

Still, it was pretty strong stuff. Would Roosevelt have accepted the plan if he had lived? We know only that Donovan thought so. He was in Paris the day Roosevelt died. One of his deputies, Colonel Ned Buxton, talked to him that evening. "What will happen now to OSS?" Buxton asked. "I'm afraid it's the end," was Donovan's reply.

He was, however, to make one more try. Shortly after V-J Day, Naval Commander John Shaheen walked into the general's office to bid him good-by. "You're not through yet," said Donovan, and he ordered Shaheen to stay in uniform for sixty more days. Shaheen sat down in mild shock while Donovan related a story. There had been that sensationalized prewar investigation of the munitions industry, conducted by Senator Gerald Nye of North Dakota, in which Donovan had acted as counsel for the Du Pont Company, one of the firms most heavily attacked. "You remember that, John? You know, John, I had to argue, not just the merits but against the whole propaganda campaign and that campaign was Gerald Nye's *Merchants of Death*. I tell you John, I learned something. Now let's see if you can do as well for OSS as Nye did for the isolationists."

Shaheen rose. "Could your secretary get me a list of writers in OSS who happen to be in Washington?"

For weeks, a series of sensational stories dominated the newspapers and magazines hailing the exploits of OSS's secret war. As Shaheen and his assistants scoured the files, had the facts declassified, fed them to "writers in OSS who happened to be in Washington," and as they fed them in turn to eager journalists, OSS parachutists returning from their hitherto secret war and expecting to hear the usual jibes about "Oh So Social" suddenly found themselves figures of glamor. But the new President, Harry Truman, was annoyed. On September 20, 1945, the publicity campaign was cut short. Truman signed Executive Order 9621, "Termination of the Office of Strategic Services and Disposition of Its Functions."

While the pro-OSS publicity was at its height, Donovan had written a letter announcing his wish to return to private life. "Therefore, in considering the disposition to be made of the assets created by OSS, I speak as a private

citizen concerned only with the security of my country."

Thirty years later, it seems odd that this last plea for his old outfit should have been addressed not to the President of the United States but to Harold B. Smith, Director of the Bureau of the Budget. But it was, at the time, not at all an odd thing to do.

As the war ended and the mind of Harry Truman turned to problems of demobilization and reorganization for peace, Harold B. Smith became for a few weeks a very powerful man. He was the one man to whom Truman could turn who knew where everything was and where it had been before. Moreover, he had a tidy housekeeper's view about what to do with it now. OSS appalled the neat-minded Smith. Here was an agency which was part research, part spies, part propaganda, part paratroopers, part saboteurs and forgers, all mixed up together in such

Allen W. Dulles, first civilian head of the CIA. "A very good man," remarked Donovan, *"...but...he ought to be number two."*
GEORGE TAMES, *New York Times* PICTURES

fashion that it was impossible to reduce it to a chart. Smith came at once to a solution:

Put the research professors and analysts under the State Department, he advised Truman; put the spies and propagandists and forgers under the War Department and let the paratroopers and saboteurs go home. For the next four

7

months, the Smith formula of separated functions of State and War became the United States intelligence establishment. Donovan, when he heard about the new formula, called it "absurd."

In the State Department, Secretary James Byrnes, acting upon the President's written instructions to "take the lead in organizing peacetime intelligence," turned the action over to Dean Acheson, who brought in Colonel Alfred McCormack, an able lawyer from New York who had served G-2 during the war. Valiantly, McCormack tried to organize a research and analytical intelligence branch in State. Opposition came not only from G-2 and ONI but from within the State Department itself. Desk officers of the Foreign Service, certain that the idea was an assault upon their authority and an insult to their expertise, reacted vigorously. In a forecast of an era to come, they succeeded in sinking the effort in a debate about whether one of the OSS men who had been brought into the department was or was not a Communist.

In his memoirs, Dean Acheson described the rout as the story of how the Department of State "muffed the intelligence role," and placed the blame on Byrnes, for whom, he said, "ideas of organization were not congenial." Eventually, McCormack resigned, and the unit he had organized was split into seventeen committees. Gradually, it wasted away.

In the War Department, the Smith formula worked a little better. There, Colonel William Quinn, a tough, open-faced man who radiated a bustling confidence—Allen Dulles called it the Donovan spirit—kept intact the spies and forgers, grouped together now under a new name, the Strategic Services Unit, or SSU. Quinn was a rarity among regular army officers because he had worked closely with OSS during the war and had admired the job it had done for him. Quinn had been G-2 of the Seventh Army during the invasion of southern France and had made good use of the OSS agents (mostly German prisoners of war) whom OSS had infiltrated behind the German lines

President Harry Truman talks over cold-war problems in 1946 with Secretary of State James Byrnes and Lieutenant General Walter Bedell Smith. Smith had recently been named U.S. Ambassador to Russia; in 1950 he became Dulles' predecessor as CIA Director.

to pick up order of battle information.

"Preserve the assets and eliminate the liabilities," Assistant Secretary of War Howard C. Petersen had told Quinn when Quinn took over SSU from retiring Brigadier General John Magruder; and among the assets Quinn counted intelligence networks in eastern Europe, Austria, the Balkans, and China. To preserve these networks, he had to hold on to the men who ran them.

There was James Angleton; there was Hugh Cunningham; there was Frank Wisner; there was Richard Helms; there was Harry Rossitzke. These were the men who over the next fifteen years were to conceive and manage the major U.S. intelligence operations against the Soviet Union. Wisner, who as CIA's Deputy Director of Plans was destined to become their chief, was the only one Quinn could not keep happy. He quit in a huff—to return some years later—because Quinn on a particular occasion refused to provide him with an additional two hundred bicycles for the agents Wisner had hired to peddle into East Germany, take a look at the Russian occupation, and report back what they learned.

Quinn had other problems. G-2, and newspaper columnists Joseph Alsop and Harold Ickes, the former Interior Secretary, suggested that Quinn's unit harbored Communists. But Quinn quickly established good relations with J. Edgar Hoover, and Hoover, having nothing to fear now from Donovan, came forward to say that he had checked the employees of SSU and found them "clean."

Whenever Quinn felt sorely threatened, he would call David Bruce, Donovan's wartime deputy for Europe, and Bruce would invite members of the old OSS hierarchy to dinner at his Washington home. Charles Cheston would arrive from Philadelphia, Donovan and Russell Forgan from New York, and they would discuss strategy for keeping the unit intact. "Without Quinn," Allen Dulles would later remark, "our profession would have lost many of its pros."

While McCormack was losing in the State Department and Quinn was hanging on in the War Department, Truman was complaining to Admiral Leahy, his chief of staff, that too many intelligence reports from State, ONI, and G-2 were cluttering his desk, and Leahy was putting pressure on Byrnes to do something about it. It was Byrnes's failure to do something about it that led to the next move around the circle.

Even as he was ordering the dissolution of OSS in 1945, President Truman was telling intimates that we needed a peacetime intelligence agency. "I was in his office one afternoon right after the war ended—I believe it was in August," his former naval aide, Clark Clifford, recalls, "when he began to talk to me about Joe Grew's cables." (Joseph Grew had been U.S. Ambassador to Japan at the time of Pearl Harbor.) "You go back and read Joe Grew," Truman said to Clifford, "and then you come in here and tell me how anybody could have read those cables and not known there was an attack coming." He proceeded to list what he considered to have been other warnings of Japanese intent. Clifford recalls that Truman knew a lot about the amount of scrap iron the Japanese were buying before Pearl Harbor. The new President concluded his lecture, according to Clifford, as follows: "If we had had some central repository for information, and somebody to look at it and fit all the pieces together, there never would have been a Pearl Harbor."

Within a few weeks Truman decided that under the plan suggested by his budget director, Harold Smith, nobody was fitting all the pieces together. His complaint to Admiral Leahy was reflected in the note Secretary of the Navy James Forrestal placed in his diary in October, 1945:

"Mr. Byrnes next raised the question of a central intelligence agency . . . responsible to a Council of Defense which would consist of the Secretaries of State, War and Navy. . . . All of the secretaries (Robert Patterson, Secretary of War, Byrnes, and Forrestal) agreed with the principle of the proposal, that any central intelligence agency should report to the three Secretaries rather than directly to the President."

The Byrnes proposal was exactly what Forrestal wanted to hear, so much so, that one suspects he arranged with Leahy to feed the idea to Byrnes in such a way that Byrnes might project it as his own. Forrestal was then engaged in a fierce struggle with the Army over a proposal to merge the two services. Desperately, he was casting about for ways to avoid it.

As a basis for argument, he had hit upon the idea that Winston Churchill's war cabinet was the way to run things: "An inner council of the most important and trusted advisers," he put it, "to care for problems of common concern." In addition, he had asked his close friend and former partner, Ferdinand Eberstadt, to make "a thorough study of postwar organization of the military services." Not surprisingly, Eberstadt echoed the idea of coordination rather than merger. The second chapter of Eberstadt's report was entitled, simply, "Intelligence." It came out strongly for a central intelligence agency which would not attempt to direct the services of the Army and Navy but which would deal with "problems of common concern," would "coordinate" and "synthesize."

"How often," Dean Acheson later wrote, "those same dismal words . . . issued from the White House during the war in order to 'clarify' various powers, functions and responsibilities . . . a good many of us had cut our teeth and throats with this sort of nonsense. We had learned that no committee can govern and no man can administer without his own people, money and authority."

Three who watched over the gestation of the CIA: top to bottom, Rear Admiral Sidney Souers, Lieutenant General Hoyt Vandenberg, and Rear Admiral Roscoe Hillenkoetter

recommended him; he had promised to stay only six months, and at the end of that time he left. But even within that short period Souers was to find that his mandate "to correlate, evaluate and plan for the coordination of . . ." was a mushy task. Just before he left, he asked for a budget of his own to be provided by the three departments he was trying to serve. He was turned down.

In June, 1946, the handsome Lieutenant General Hoyt Vandenberg, Air Force ace and nephew of the most powerful Republican in the Senate, Arthur S. Vandenberg of Michigan, succeeded to Souers' job. Vandenberg wanted very much to be the first Chief of Staff of the Air Force and was not inclined to rock any boats on the way to the job. Nevertheless, his title, his looks, and his relationship to the senator, as well as his high abilities, gave him authority Souers had lacked. Despite opposition from Byrnes and Patterson, he succeeded in getting a specific allocation of money for the CIG, in replacing the FBI as the intelligence collection agency in South America, and in winning the right to conduct research and analysis independent of the military services. Most important, Vandenberg took over Quinn's SSU, thus acquiring a clandestine collection capability and, incidentally, sending Quinn off to the Army War College for a leg up on what would be a highly successful army career.

But Vandenberg like Souers wanted to leave quickly, and when in May, 1947, he won the top Air Force job, he turned over CIG to a lackluster leader, Rear Admiral Roscoe H. Hillenkoetter.

Hillenkoetter never seemed to be quite sure whether he was more interested in foreign intelligence or domestic communism. He liked to pore over long lists of people in and out of government whom he suspected of being left-wing, and then issue memoranda forbidding CIG employees to "have any communication with the Following." Nevertheless, he holds the honor of being the only American ever to head both the Central Intelligence Group and the Central Intelligence Agency, and when he left in 1950 to assume a sea command, the groundwork for what was to become an enormous intelligence and covert-action bureaucracy had been laid.

Still, Harry Truman could not have been pleased by the change he had set in motion. Separate intelligence reports from G-2, ONI, and the State Department continued to flow across his desk. The new CIG merely added one more. But the military intelligence services had not wanted the CIG and had indeed fought hard against it. Only the agreement between Patterson and Forrestal had carried the day. Perhaps Truman thought that real change would come when the armed services unification bill was finally passed, and a more powerful intelligence agency could take its place in the new organization that would emerge.

Acheson had learned. But Forrestal had not. And so, on January 22, 1946, Truman, forsaking the Smith plan, directed, by executive letter to Byrnes, the establishment of a new National Intelligence Authority. It would consist of the Secretaries of State, War, and the Navy, and would possess, as its operating arm, something called the Central Intelligence Group. The man on top would be Director of Central Intelligence. He would have no money of his own, no people of his own, and no authority except the high-sounding title.

As the first Director of Central Intelligence Truman chose Rear Admiral Sidney Souers, who in private life was a St. Louis businessman. I recall an interview with Admiral Souers shortly after he took office. "What do you want to do?" I asked the new appointee. The admiral looked up from behind Donovan's old desk and chuckled: "I want to go home," he replied.

Contrary to assumptions at the time, Souers was not a Truman crony, though he later became one. Forrestal had

"An intelligence agency was the tail," Clark Clifford says

of the establishment of CIA. "The entire defense establishment spent 1946 and part of 1947 arguing about the National Security Act. How should we merge the Army and the Navy and establish the Air Force and what should be the powers of the Secretary of Defense, and what should be the mission and the authority of each service? That was the dog. Nobody paid much attention to the intelligence part of the bill."

Indeed, the drafters of the unification act planned it that way. The CIG legislative counsel, Walter Pforzheimer, went to the White House one day with two copies of draft legislation. The first authorized a CIA. The second authorized covert and unvouchered funds for the CIA. In a meeting with Admiral Forrest Sherman, who was handling unification legislation for the Navy, General Lorris Norstadt, who was doing the same for the Army, and White House counsel Charles Murphy, Pforzheimer was told to forget about the second draft. "They thought," he recalls, "that the secret funding would open up a can of worms, and delay unification. We could come up with the house-keeping provisions later on."

And so the CIA was born. "A small but elite corps of men with a passion for anonymity and a willingness to stick to the job." That was Allen Dulles' description to Congress of what he thought the agency should be. General of the Army Dwight D. Eisenhower also testified, and some thought that his remarks pointed to Dulles.

"One of the difficulties," said Eisenhower, doubtless thinking of the military attachés of G-2 for whom he had more than once expressed contempt, "is getting a man who will understand intelligence. He must show a bent for it and be trained all the way up. If I could get the civilian I wanted, and knew he would stay for ten years, I would be content, myself."

There was almost no opposition to the intelligence portion of the act. Congressman Clare Hoffman of Michigan wanted an amendment to bar the new agency from "the collection of intelligence." Hoffman represented G-2's last stand. Congressman Walter H. Judd of Minnesota introduced an amendment that would "prevent this agency from being allowed to go in and inspect J. Edgar Hoover's activities and work." Judd represented the FBI's last stand. Neither of the amendments was adopted.

When it was all over—the date was July 26, 1947—the nation's newspapers headlined the fact that Congress had passed the National Security Act. The armed services were to be "unified" under a new Department of Defense. Far down in its account of the historic event, the *New York Times* reported that "there will also be a Central Intelligence Agency." Donovan read the account and remarked to a friend, "I see they finally made intelligence respectable."

The National Security Act of 1947 gave the Central Intelligence Agency power to hire its own people and to

have its own budget, though it was not yet to be a secret, unvouchered budget. The legislation made the new agency responsible to a new National Security Council (Forrestal's vehicle for handling problems of "common concern"). Apart from this change, CIA was a continuation of CIG, its powers and functions recited in almost the same language in which President Truman had enumerated the powers and functions of CIG in the letter he had written to Byrnes back in 1946.

Donovan, who had not been called to testify on the act, noted this fact. "Those fellows don't know what they're doing," he remarked, "because they're not sure what they can do." It was not quite an accurate statement. "Those fellows" knew they could spy. They had been spying for CIG under the authority "to perform for the benefit of existing agencies . . . services of common concern." This language from Truman's 1946 directive was now incorporated into law, and the legislative history makes it clear that Congress knew what the language meant.

On the other hand, the question of whether Congress authorized what Donovan had once called "subversive operations abroad" is less clear. The weight of evidence suggests that it did not. But the legislation did contain the following clause, also carried over from the Truman directive that had set up CIG: ". . . perform such other functions and duties related to intelligence affecting the national security as the National Security Council may from time to time direct."

This was Donovan language—straight out of his 1945 memorandum to Roosevelt, though slightly amended by Clark Clifford, who had inserted after the word "Intelligence" the words "affecting the national security" and had

Secretary of Defense James Forrestal, 1947

11

...and how it grew: At left is one of the modest buildings in Washington, D.C., originally occupied by the CIA after its start in 1947. In 1961 the organization, enormously expanded, moved to the massive complex below, photographed from the air at Langley, Virginia.

thought of it at the time as "a restricting clause." But Donovan had never intended "such other functions and duties" as any more than a catchall. It was later—about a year later—before it occurred to anyone that "such other functions and duties" might be construed to mean "subversive operations abroad."

One day early in 1948, Admiral Hillenkoetter, who was still in charge, called CIA's general counsel, Lawrence Houston, into his office and asked him a question. Could CIA spend money to help defeat the Communist Party in the upcoming Italian elections? Houston remembers that Hillenkoetter said he had been talking to James Forrestal, the new Secretary of Defense. "I've looked all over the government and I can't find anybody who can do it," Forrestal had said to him. "Can you fellows do it?"

Houston told Hillenkoetter he doubted the new agency had that authority. Then he went back to his office, got out the legislation, and reread it. There it was: "such other functions and duties . . . ." He thought about it, and decided that it did not constitute congressional authorization to spend money to influence an election in a foreign country. He informed Hillenkoetter that this was his opinion.

But the point had been raised, and now it became an arguable one. Forrestal and Hillenkoetter disagreed with Houston. So did Harry Truman. The CIA decided that it would conduct the Italian operation; and it was a turning point. Suddenly, down the road—with presidential approval—the lights turned green.

———————————

On a late winter's day in 1954, United States Ambassador to Thailand William J. Donovan paid his last official visit to the CIA. By that time the agency was almost precisely what Donovan had envisaged that his peacetime OSS would become. If the relatively overt intelligence and analysis side of the house was not performing as Donovan had intended, if there was still duplication in reporting and overlapping with the armed services and State, the secret side of the house had more than compensated.

All over the world there were networks and agents in place, and both at home and abroad "other functions and duties" were being carried out. Paratroopers were in training; newspapers, radio stations, magazines, airlines, ships, businesses, and voluntary organizations had been bought, subsidized, penetrated, or invented as assets for the cold war. In terms of manpower alone, the agency was already bigger than Donovan's wartime OSS had been, and it was spending more money than General Donovan, an imaginative man, may have imagined.

"The sums made available to the Agency may be expended without regard to the provision of law," said the CIA Act of 1949. ". . . such expenditures to be accounted for solely on the certificate of the Director and every such certificate shall be deemed a sufficient voucher. . . ."

Admiral Hillenkoetter had presided over congressional approval of this language, and had then handed over his office to Lieutenant General Walter Bedell Smith, the irascible sergeant who had risen to become Eisenhower's chief of staff during World War II. Then had come war in Korea and good reason to do what Smith wanted to do, which was to centralize, expand, and bring in the promised civilian head who would stay for ten years.

Smith had had half his stomach removed, and the operation had not improved his temper. "Dulles," he would roar through the open door to his new deputy's office, "Dulles, Goddamnit, get in here." But there was never any doubt—except perhaps in the mind of Bill Donovan— that Smith respected Dulles and that Dulles would get his job.

It was an odd meeting that Donovan attended in 1954 on the occasion of his last call, partly ceremonial and partly business. Most of the deputies and division chiefs who had served under him were there, and the meeting was given additional emphasis by the presence of Frank Wisner, who supervised all covert operations from his office of Deputy Director of Plans, as well as of Dulles himself.

From a chair facing a semicircle of juniors, Donovan made his plea. He wanted money—quite a lot of money— in order to fight the Communist guerrillas in Thailand and he knew how the battle should be waged. "All I'm asking for is a bowl of rice in their bellies and a gun in their hands," he said, referring to a hoped-for army of counterinsurgents.

So there they all were—former subalterns risen to high responsibility, hearing once more from the Old Man and hating it mightily. The things he was talking about were already afoot, through the responsible government of Thailand. Each of those present had at least some small piece of the action and each dreaded the thought that the complicated work might be further complicated by having to deal with Wild Bill Donovan as a kind of third force.

When Donovan finished, there was polite applause. Hands were shaken all round and Dulles took the visitor off for a private chat. Years later, one of those who was present thought to inquire about the outcome. "What did you ever do," he asked Dulles, "about Bill Donovan's last request?"

Dulles smiled reflectively. "I arranged for him to have a very capable assistant," he answered, "so that I knew exactly what he was doing—and then I gave him some of what he wanted."

"You know," he added, and his eyes took on that familiar "this-is-in-confidence" look, "it wouldn't have been right for us to turn Bill down altogether."

———————————

Tom Braden was for many years the editor and publisher of the Oceanside, California, Blade Tribune, *and is now active in and around Washington, D.C. With the late Stewart Alsop he was the co-author of* Sub Rosa: The OSS and American Espionage.

THE TRANSCONTINENTAL RAILROAD

by Dee Brown

What it was like for the first travelers

Although Indians harassed the builders of the Union Pacific, they tended to shun the line by 1872, when this lurid lithograph was published by the Boston house of Haskell & Allen. Nevertheless, there was adventure enough waiting for anyone who went west by the steam cars.

14

I see over my own continent the Pacific railroad surmounting every barrier,
I see continual trains of cars winding along the Platte carrying freight and passengers,
I hear the locomotives rushing and roaring, and the shrill steamwhistle,
I hear the echoes reverberate through the grandest scenery in the world . . .
Bridging the three or four thousand miles of land travel,
Tying the Eastern to the Western sea . . .

—Walt Whitman, *Passage to India.*

On May 15, 1869, regular train service began on America's first transcontinental railroad. Thousands of Americans who had become accustomed to train travel in the Eastern states could now journey behind an iron horse all the way to Walt Whitman's Western sea. Although it was not possible—except in cases of special excursions—to board a car in an Eastern city and journey uninterrupted to California, most of these pioneer travelers seemed to look upon the necessary transfers in Chicago and Omaha, and Promontory or Ogden, as welcome breaks in an eight to ten days adventure.

"Every man who could command the time and money was eager to make the trip," declared that energetic traveling reporter John Beadle, "and everybody who could sling ink became correspondents." From the very beginning, many travelers did indeed seem compelled to make a written record of their experiences. Their accounts were usually very sketchy until they passed Chicago or Omaha. During the first year of transcontinental service, passengers from the East arrived in Chicago on the Michigan Central Railroad, but by the mid-1870's they had their choice of connections from the Pennsylvania, Erie, or New York Central.

"Seventy-five minutes are allowed for getting from the station of arrival to the station of departure," said William F. Rae, an Englishman who made the journey late in 1869. "In my own case the times of the trains did not correspond; the one train had started an hour before the other arrived." Because he had planned to stop over briefly in Chicago, Rae was not disappointed by the enforced delay of twenty-four hours, but many of his fellow passengers were, and for another century travelers through Chicago would continue to suffer the inconvenience of changing trains and failure to make connections. During the heyday of American railroad passenger travel, one of the common sayings was that a hog could travel across country through Chicago without changing cars, but a human being could not.

To reach the Union Pacific from Chicago, travelers had their choice of two direct routes, the Rock Island or the Northwestern, and an indirect route, the Chicago, Burlington & Quincy. Knowledgeable people taking the direct routes soon learned to avoid the evening express trains which left them stranded in Council Bluffs or Omaha for almost twenty-four hours while they awaited the departure of the U.P.'s daily train for the Pacific Coast.

Until a bridge was completed across the Missouri River in 1872, westbound travelers also had to endure a crossing in a ferryboat from Council Bluffs to Omaha. And even after the bridge was built, the railroads refused to be cooperative enough to take the cars of the Eastern roads across the river to the Union Pacific station. Arriving in Council Bluffs, passengers had to remove themselves and their baggage to the cars of the Transfer Company. John Erastus Lester of Providence, Rhode Island, who traveled west in 1872 in hopes of improving his health, said that passage by the Transfer Company "caused more hard words to be spoken than can be erased from the *big book* for many a day." He was not only disenchanted by the company's treatment of passengers but by its requirement that all freight be unloaded from Eastern cars and then repacked for shipment across the river.

Early travelers on the transcontinental railroad saw little to admire about Omaha. One found it to be "the muddiest place I ever saw," but added that "the roads are generally deep with dust." Another also described the town as being layered with mud through which "the omnibus labored slowly, the outside passengers being advised by the driver to move about from one side of the roof to another, in order to guard against upsetting the overloaded vehicle. A general feeling of relief was manifested when the station of the Union Pacific Railway was reached."

Almost all agreed they had seldom seen such bustling confusion as developed at the Omaha station at the times for train departures. During the early years when the journey west was considered a daring enterprise, rumors were deliberately spread among the greenhorn ticket buyers of danger from wild Indians wrecking or attacking trains; this of course aided the Omaha railroad agents in the sale of insurance policies for the journey.

Except for a quick whistle from the engine and the conductor's cry of "All aboard!" there was no warning of the train's departure. This usually resulted in a rush of passengers who had to hop on board the moving cars. "For three or four miles we pass along the bluffs on which Omaha is built," John Lester recorded, "and then push out upon the open prairie, the fertile lands of Nebraska. A vast plain, dotted here and there with trees, stretches away upon every side."

In springtime the rolling land was covered with wildflowers whose fragrance drifted into the open windows of cars moving along at twenty miles an hour; in summer tumbleweeds by the thousands wheeled across the drying grass; and by autumn prairie fires blazed against the horizon. "The spectacle of a prairie on fire is one of infinite grandeur," said William Rae. "For miles on every side the air is heavy with volumes of stifling smoke, and the ground reddened with hissing and rushing fire."

Travelers from abroad found the Great Plains grass to be shorter than they had expected, and they compared the wind-driven sweep of grayish green to ocean waves, "undulating like the Atlantic with a heavy groundswell." They also complained of their eyes wearying at the sameness of landscape, of the train seeming to be standing still in an immense void. All welcomed the first break in the monotony of the plains—the Platte River, which the railroad followed westward as had the wagon trains of earlier years.

When the transcontinental railroad opened for service, George Mortimer Pullman had been manufacturing experimental models of his sleeping cars for four years, and the Union Pacific accepted several of them in 1869. They were called Pullman Palace Cars and their exteriors were painted in rich brown colors to distinguish them from the drab coaches. Everyone who could afford the additional $25 for first-class fare and $4 per day for a Pullman Palace Car was eager to obtain a berth. First-class travelers paid $100 for the journey from Omaha to Sacramento; second-class or coach $75. There was also a special rate of $40 for immigrants, who rode on cramped board seats. Four to five days were usually required to complete the journey by express, six to seven days by mixed train. The speed of trains varied according to the conditions of tracks and bridges, dropping to nine miles per hour over hastily built sections and increasing to thirty-five miles per hour over smoother tracks. Most travelers of the early 1870's mentioned eighteen to twenty-two miles per hour as the average. Although speeds were doubled within a decade, time-consuming stops and starts at more than two hundred stations and water tanks prevented any considerable reduction in total hours spent on the long journey.

Even in an era when the most highly skilled Americans earned less than $100 a month, demand for hundred-dollar Pullman space on the transcontinental railroad was so great that the Union Pacific began running three sleeping cars on some trains early in 1870 and was still turning away would-be ticket buyers. Because of George Pullman's interest in the Union Pacific, he supplied that railroad with de luxe innovations long before they reached the Eastern roads. Travelers heard or read about the Palace Cars and were eager to ride on them no matter what the cost. "I had a sofa to myself, with a table and a lamp," wrote one satisfied rider. "The sofas are widened and made into beds at night. My berth was three feet three inches wide, and six feet three inches long. It had two windows looking out of the train, a handsome mirror, and was well furnished with bedding and curtains."

British travelers were especially impressed, and sent off earnest letters to railway directors in London urging them "to take a leaf out of the Americans' book, and provide sleeping carriages for long night journeys." They also delighted in the freedom of movement from one car to another, although the traveler who signed himself "A London Parson" admitted that trying to dress one's self in a box two feet high was a bit inconvenient. "It was an odd experience, that going to bed of some thirty ladies,

gentlemen, and children, in, practically, one room. For two nights I had a young married couple sleeping in the berth above mine. The lady turned in first, and presently her gown was hung out over the rail to which her bed curtains were fastened. But further processes of unrobing were indicated by the agitation of the drapery which concealed her nest. As the same curtain served for both berths—hers and mine—the gentleman held her portion together over my head when it was necessary for me to retire. At last all were housed, and some snores rose above the rattle of the train. I did not sleep much the first night, but looked over the moonlit prairie from my pillow."

Although Pullman introduced a "hotel car" in 1870 with a kitchen at one end from which meals were served on removable tables set between the drawing-room seats, the Union Pacific scheduled the car for only one trip each week. Until well into the 1880's the transcontinental railroad fed its passengers at dining stations along the way, allowing them thirty minutes to obtain their food and bolt it down before resuming the journey.

Judging from comments of travelers, the food varied from wretched to middling fair. The first dining stop out of Omaha was Grand Island. "Ill cooked and poorly served," was one passenger's blunt comment. "We found the quality on the whole bad," said William Robertson of Scotland, "and all three meals, breakfast, dinner and supper, were almost identical, viz., tea, buffalo steaks, antelope chops, sweet potatoes, and boiled Indian corn, with hoe cakes and syrup *ad nauseam.*" New Yorker Susan Coolidge also complained about the sameness of diet. "It was necessary to look at one's watch to tell whether it was breakfast, dinner or supper that we were eating, these meals presenting invariably the same salient features of beefsteak, fried eggs, fried potato." She was generous enough to compliment the chef at Sidney, Nebraska, for serving "cubes of fried mush which diversified a breakfast of unusual excellence." Harvey Rice of Cleveland, Ohio, described the Sidney breakfast station as a crude structure of boards and canvas. "Here the passengers were replenished with an excellent breakfast—a chicken stew, as they supposed, but which, as they were afterward informed, consisted of prairie-dogs—a new variety of chickens, without feathers. This information created an unpleasant sensation in sundry delicate stomachs."

According to William L. Humason of Hartford, Connecticut, the farther one traveled across the plains the worse the dining stations became, "consisting of miserable shanties, with tables dirty, and waiters not only dirty, but saucy. The tea tasted as though it were made from the leaves of the sage-brush—literally *sage tea*. The biscuit was made without soda, but with plenty of alkali, harmonizing with the great quantity of alkali dust we had already swallowed." The only dining station Humason had a good word for was at Cisco, California, where the water on the table was as clear as crystal, but he thought a dollar and a quarter was "a pretty steep price to pay for fried ham and potatoes."

At most dining stops, meal prices were one dollar, and

16

on the California section of the Central Pacific the prices were reduced to seventy-five cents if the diner paid in silver rather than in paper money. Neither the Union Pacific nor the Central Pacific operated their eating houses, preferring to contract them to private individuals, with no required standard of service. Most of them were in rough frame buildings filled with long tables upon which large platters of food were waiting when passengers descended from the trains. Gradually the individual stations achieved reputations for certain specialties such as beefsteak at Laramie, hot biscuits at Green River, antelope at Sidney, fish at Colfax. The most frequently praised dining stop was Evanston, Wyoming, where mountain trout was the specialty. "It was kept by a colored man named Howard W. Crossley whose evident desire was to please all," wrote John Lester. He added that most "proprietors of the eating-stations ought to be promoted to higher callings; for they are evidently above running a hotel."

Because Cheyenne was listed in the guidebooks as the largest city between Omaha and Sacramento, many passengers expected a superior quality of food service there. They were disappointed to find a small town of board and canvas buildings occupied (as one wrote) by about three thousand "dangerous-looking miners in big boots, broad-brimmed hats, and revolvers." The only added feature in the dining station was a formidable row of heads of big-game animals which glared down from the walls upon the famished passengers. "The chops were generally as tough as hanks of whipcord, and the knives as blunt as bricklayers' trowels," one traveler reported.

Between stops for meals the passengers were diverted by a procession of unfamiliar wildlife along each side of the track, antelope and prairie dogs being the most commonly seen. Far more antelope than buffalo ranged along the Union Pacific tracks, and long files of these fleet-footed animals often approached very close to passing trains, apparently racing with the cars, and usually winning. Although the Union Pacific frowned upon the practice, eager hunters sometimes fired upon these animals with rifles and pistols from the open windows of the cars. Few hits were recorded.

Prairie-dog villages also were close enough so that passengers could observe these gregarious rodents sitting at the entrances to their burrows. "They fling themselves in the air with a gay nimbleness beautiful to see, flip a somersault, and present to the admiring gaze of the traveler two furry heels and a short furry tail as they make their exit from the stage of action," wrote one passenger.

Elk, wolves, and bears were often seen as the iron horse thundered across the West, and one traveler was sure that he saw a pack of wild dogs trotting along parallel with the railroad, until he learned that they were coyotes. Swarms

In 1877 the publisher Frank Leslie set off from New York to cover the transcontinental journey for his Illustrated Newspaper. *Though Leslie traveled in a flossy Wagner Drawing-Room Car, he deigned to explore the other cars, and the sketches he ran in his paper are one of the best records of life on the overland train.*

When the harrowing twenty-minute meal stops gave way to dining cars, travelers ate in more comfort—and better. The tiny kitchens miraculously produced elaborate meals, which were consumed, said one of Leslie's party, "with an appetite unknown east of Missouri."

Frank Leslie's Illustrated Newspaper

of grasshoppers and crickets were another unfamiliar sight; they sometimes descended upon the tracks and caused the locomotive wheels to spin into a temporary stall.

Although only thinning herds of buffalo remained near the Union Pacific right-of-way after train travel began, the iron horses of the Kansas Pacific (which ran less than two hundred miles to the south and connected with the Union Pacific at Cheyenne) occasionally were surrounded by buffalo and had to slow down or wait until the herd passed. One traveler on the Kansas Pacific told of seeing a herd that extended as far as the eye could reach. "With heads down and tails up they galloped towards the track making extraordinary exertions to get across ahead of the locomotive. In trying this strategic feat one specimen found himself forcibly lifted into the air and thrown into the ditch, where he lay upon his back, his cloven feet flourishing madly."

In its early days, before connections were scheduled with other railroads, the Kansas Pacific engineers willingly stopped trains to permit the passengers to leave the cars and shoot at passing buffalo. "Everybody runs out and commences shooting," lawyer John Putnam of Topeka wrote a friend in 1868. "We failed to bag a buffalo. I did not shoot, having ill defined ideas as to hunting rifles, which end you put the load in and which end you let it out at . . . But I rushed out with the rest—yelled promiscuously—'Buffalo!—Stop the train'—'let me out'—'there they are!—Whoop-pey'—'Give 'em thunder'—'no go'—'Come back'—'drive on'— So you see I helped a good deal."

The buffalo and other animals entertained the travelers against a constantly changing background of scenery which grew more and more fascinating as they left the plains behind. The first glimpse of the snowy range of the Rocky Mountains always sent a wave of excitement through the passenger cars. "My boyish dreams were realized," one man recorded. "For hours, at the school desk, have I pondered over the map and wandered, in imagination, with Lewis and Clark, the hunters and trappers and early emigrants, away off to these Rocky Mountains, about which such a mystery seemed to hang,—dreaming, wishing and hoping against hope, that my eyes might, some day, behold their snow-crowned heights. And here lay the first great range in the pureness of white; distant, to be sure, but there it lay, enshrined in beauty."

Wyoming was filled with wonders for these journeyers from the East, but when the iron horse brought them through tunnels into Utah's Echo and Weber canyons, they were at a loss for superlatives to describe the towering castlelike rocks. "Grand beyond description . . . castles in the air . . . fantastic shapes and profiles . . . the scene is as fearful as it is sublime." Shortly after entering the Narrows of Weber Canyon, virtually everyone made note of the Thousand-mile Tree, a single green pine in a desolation of rock and sage, marking the distance from Omaha. European travelers compared Weber Canyon to gateways to the Alps. Castle Rock, Hanging Rock, Pulpit Rock, Devil's Gate, Devil's Slide—all entered the notebooks of

scribbling passengers who seemed to disagree as to whether they were creations of God or Satan.

Along the way were occasional reminders of pioneers of a previous day—the bones of long-dead oxen and horses beside the deep-rutted trails where covered wagons had crawled, a solitary grave marker, a broken wheel, a piece of discarded furniture. "Inch by inch, the teams toiled to gain a higher foothold," said one appreciative train traveler, "inch by inch they *climbed* down the rugged passes; *now* in luxurious coaches, with horses of iron, with a skilled engineer for a driver we are carried along in comfort."

When there were no animals or scenery to entertain or awe, there was always the ever-changing weather of the West. The train on which Harvey Rice was journeying to California in 1869 ran through a typically violent Great Plains thunderstorm. "The heavens became, suddenly, as black as starless midnight. The lightning flashed in every direction, and electric balls of fire rolled over the plains. It seemed as if the artillery of heaven had made the valley a target and that we were doomed to instant destruction. But happily our fears were soon dissipated. The storm was succeeded by a brilliant rainbow."

Heavy rains were likely to flood the tracks, and in the early years before roadbeds were well ballasted the ties sank into the mud. One traveler was startled to see the car behind him churning up such a foam of mud that it resembled a boat rushing along on water. It was not unusual for hailstorms to break car windows, and tornadoes could lift a train off the track. One of the legends of the Kansas Pacific concerns a tornadic waterspout that dropped out of a massive thunderstorm, washed out six thousand feet of track, and swallowed up a freight train. "Although great efforts were made to find it," said Charles B. George, a veteran railroad man, "not a trace of it has ever been discovered."

Winter travelers could expect magnificent snowstorms or fierce blizzards which sometimes turned a journey across the continent into an ordeal. On William Rae's return trip east from California in the winter of 1870, the engine pulling his train fought a two-hour battle with a snowstorm across four miles of the Laramie plains. The delay played havoc with train schedules on the single-track Union Pacific, but Rae reported that the hot-air stove in his Pullman car kept it "as comfortable as the best-warmed room in an English house."

Rae might not have been so fortunate had he been traveling on the Kansas Pacific, which suffered as severely from blizzards as it did from thunder squalls. High winds drifted both snow and sand into cuts, leveling them across the tops, and the sturdy little wood-burning locomotives would have to back up, be uncoupled from the cars, and then run at full speed into the snowbanked cuts. This was called "bucking the snow," and usually had to be repeated several times before it was effective. Engineer Cy Warman told of bucking an eighteen-foot drift with double engines so hard that his locomotive trembled and shook as if it were about to be crushed to pieces. "Often when we came to a stop only the top of the stack of the front engine would be visible. . . . All this time the snow kept coming down, day and night, until the only signs of a railroad across the range were the tops of the telegraph poles." If the passengers were lucky, the train was backed to the nearest station, but even then conditions might be harsh. A group of snowbound train travelers who crowded into a hotel in Hays City, Kansas, spent an uncomfortably cold night and at daylight found their beds covered with snow which had drifted through cracks in walls and roof.

The universal desire of all pioneer travelers on the transcontinental was to see a "real wild Indian." Few of them did, because the true warriors of the plains hated the iron horse and seldom came within miles of it. After the resisting tribes finally realized they could not stop the building of the Union Pacific's tracks, their leaders signed treaties which removed their people from the broad swaths of land taken by the railroad. As the buffalo herds also fled far to the north and south, there was no economic reason for the horse Indians to approach the tracks. The Indians that the travelers saw were mostly those who had been corrupted and weakened by contacts with the white man's civilization—scroungers, mercenaries, or beggars by necessity.

Except for a few acculturated representatives of Mississippi Valley tribes (who still plaited their hair but wore white man's clothing and frequented railroad stations from Chicago to Omaha) the westbound travelers' first glimpse of Plains Indians was around the Loup Fork in Nebraska where the Pawnees lived on a reservation. Although the Pawnees had virtually abandoned their horse-buffalo culture and lived off what they could cadge from white men, the warriors still shaved their heads to a tuft, painted their faces, and wore feathers and blankets. To travelers fresh from the East the Pawnees had a very bloodthirsty appearance, and according to the guidebooks every one of them had several scalps waving from the tops of lodgepoles.

Anywhere across western Nebraska or Wyoming, a traveler might catch a quick glimpse of a passing Sioux, Cheyenne, Arapaho, or Crow staring at the iron horse, but they were few and far between. Not until the train reached Nevada was there a plenitude of Shoshones and Paiutes hanging about every station and using their treaty rights with the Central Pacific to ride the cars back and forth. Because these desert Indians were generally covered with dust and were often unbathed (there was no water readily available), the fastidious passengers found them objectionable, and the Central Pacific gradually put restrictions on their use of trains. At first they were confined to the emigrants' coaches, and then after the emigrants objected to their presence, the Indians had to ride in the baggage cars or outside on the boarding steps.

Despite these docile remnants of the Great Plains tribes, some travelers spent a good deal of time worrying about Indian attacks. But train wrecks, and not ambushes, were the most immediate danger. Because of the relatively slow speeds of the early years, bruises rather than fatalities were the likely results unless the accident occurred on a high bridge or mountain shoulder. Poor tracks and hot boxes (overheating of axle bearings) caused many wrecks, and a surprising number of passengers suffered injuries from falling or jumping out of open car windows. One of the pioneer passengers of 1869 recorded how it felt to be in a train wreck in Echo Canyon: "On we bounded over the ties, the car wheels breaking many of them as though they were but pipe-stems. Every instant we expected to roll down the ravine. We ordered the ladies to cling to the sides of the seats and keep their feet clear of the floor. It seemed as if that train could never be stopped! But it was brought to a standstill upon the brink of an embankment. Had the cars gone a few rods further the reader would probably never have been troubled by these hastily written pages."

Still another westbound traveler during that first year told of being shaken out of his seat when a Central Pacific train ran into a herd of cattle between Wadsworth and Clark's Station, Nevada. The collision threw the locomotive off the track, but a telegrapher aboard climbed the nearest pole, tapped the line, and summoned a relief engine. During the eight-hour delay the hungry passengers butchered the dead cattle, built a fire, and cooked steaks. Such encounters with cattle were among the most common causes of train wrecks in the West, and railroad men and ranchers were in constant friction for more than half a century over the rights of cattle to trespass on railroad property.

There were, of course, less-violent diversions than wrecks. At times on the journey, said Henry Williams in *The Pacific Tourist*, one could "sit and read, play games, and indulge in social conversation and glee." By "glee" the guidebook author probably was referring to the improvised musicales and recitations that were especially popular among the Pullman passengers. In the early 1870's some Pullman cars had organs installed on them, and in the evenings amateur musicians as well as traveling troupes of professionals willingly gave performances. As one Pullman passenger described it, "music sounds upon the prairie and dies away far over the plains; merry-making and jokes, conversation and reading pass the time pleasantly until ten o'clock, when we retire. . . . If people who are traveling together will only try to make those about them happy, then a good time is assured. The second night on the road we arranged a little entertainment in the car and invited the ladies and gentlemen from the other cars into our 'improvised Music Hall.' The exercises consisted principally of recitations, with the delineation of the characters of Grace Greenwood. . . . The young ladies sang for us; and we were all happy—for the time, at least."

It was customary on Sundays to hold religious services in one of the cars. On a train rolling through western Wyoming in 1872, John Lester read the Episcopal service, the Reverend Mr. Murray delivered a sermon entitled "To Die Is Gain," and a choir sang "Nearer, My God, To Thee" and the American national hymn. "Here in the very midst of the Rocky Mountain wilderness," wrote Lester, "our thanksgivings were offered up; and our music floated out upon the air, and resounded through the deep caverns, and among the towering hills."

According to most travelers the popular pastimes were cards, conversation, and reading. "We had an abundant supply of books and newspapers. A boy frequently traversed the train with a good store of novels, mostly English, periodicals, etc. . . . In the evening we had our section lighted, and played a solemn game of whist, or were initiated into the mysteries of euchre, or watched the rollicking game of poker being carried on by a merry party in the opposite section."

There may have been some "rollicking" poker games on Pullman cars, but most of them were as deadly serious as the real money-making endeavors of the players in that gilded age of the robber barons. Brakeman Harry French told of witnessing such a game one evening in the course of his duties. "The car was loaded to capacity with wealthy stockmen, and I suspect, a number of fancy women. In the cramped quarters of the men's smoking room, a high-play poker game was in progress. Gold pieces and bills were the stakes, and they were very much in evidence. I was particularly interested in one of the players. Fine clothes, careful barbering, diamond-decked fingers marked him as a gambler." Poker-playing professional gamblers, fresh from the declining riverboat traffic of the Mississippi River, could indeed be found on almost any transcontinental train in the 1870's, and many a greenhorn bound west to seek his fortune lost his nest egg before reaching the end of his journey.

By the time the passengers arrived at Sherman Summit on their second day out of Omaha, they had formed into the usual little groups and cliques, and knew each other by sight if not by name. Sherman Summit, the most elevated station on the Pacific railroad (the highest in the world, according to the guidebooks), was also the halfway point between Omaha and the Union Pacific's

Buffalo, like Indians, were fairly scarce along the right-of-way, but occasionally trains were held up by herds, and sometimes passengers got a chance to squeeze off a shot or two at the beasts. This scene was painted by the Philadelphia artist Newbold Trotter.

Wrapped in their American army-issue greatcoats, two off-duty Pawnee scouts watch the goings-on at a prairie depot.

described by various travelers as dreary, awful, lifeless. They complained of burning eyes and sore lips caused by the clouds of alkali dust swirled up into the cars, and thought Bitter Creek and Salt Wells appropriately descriptive names for stations.

About sunrise the train arrived at Green River for a breakfast stop, and for the next hundred miles everyone looked forward to the moment of crossing into Utah Territory, the land of the Mormons and their plural wives. Wahsatch was the noon dining station, and every passenger from the East who stepped down from the train peered expectantly around for Mormons, but the What Cheer Eating House looked about the same as all the others they had seen.

At Ogden, passengers awaiting connecting trains frequently had to spend many hours in a long narrow wooden building which had been erected between the tracks of the Union Pacific and the Central Pacific. In addition to ticket offices and a large dining room, sleeping rooms furnished only with curtains for doors were available upstairs. One Englishwoman considered her enforced stay there an adventure: "Except for the passing trains this is a most lonely, isolated spot, weird and still, lying in the heart of the mountains. In the evening a blinding snowstorm came on, and the wind, howling fearfully with a rushing mighty sound, shook the doors and rattled at the windows as though it wanted to come in and warm itself at our blazing wood fire."

Upon boarding the Central Pacific at Ogden, the first-class passengers found themselves in Silver Palace cars instead of Pullmans. Collis Huntington and his Big Four partners refused to accept George Pullman's arrangement for the use of his sleeping cars and ordered their own constructed. The Silver Palaces were attractive with their white metallic interiors, but although they were outfitted with private sitting rooms and smoking rooms, they lacked the luxurious touches which travelers from the East had grown accustomed to in their Pullmans. Passengers complained that their berths were not as roomy or as comfortable, and some said the cars were often too cold. Eventually the Central Pacific had to give up the Silver Palaces because transcontinental passengers resented having to change from their Pullmans.

The Cosmopolitan Hotel of booming Elko, Nevada, was the first dining stop west of Ogden. Alkali dust swirled in streets filled with freight wagons drawn by long mule teams hauling supplies to miners in nearby Pine Valley. Chinese workers discharged by the railroad had established a colony here and were much in evidence around the hotel. Beyond Elko was the valley of the Humboldt and the crossing of Nevada's barren deserts. In summer, passengers choked on dust if they left the windows open, or sweltered in heat if they closed them. After passing Winnemucca, the iron horse turned southward to the Humboldt Sink (where the river was literally swallowed up by the desert) and thereafter, instead of facing the sun, continued a southwesterly course to the Sierra.

By this time the passengers were beginning to show the effects of several days travel, "a drooping, withered,

end of track at Ogden. If the westbound express was on schedule, the engineer would stop his panting iron horse longer than usual at the Sherman water tank in order to give the passengers a chance to stretch their legs, inhale the rarefied air, and enjoy the view before crossing Dale Creek bridge and plunging down the mountains into Laramie for a noon meal stop.

At Sherman some passengers were afflicted with nosebleed from the height, or were badly chilled by the cold wind, and were glad to leave it behind. Others found it inspiring: "Never till this moment did I realize the truthfulness of Bierstadt's scenery of these hills. The dark, deep shadows, the glistening sides, and the snow-capped peaks, with their granite faces, the stunted growth of pine and cedar, all render the scene such as he has painted it." And another traveler, Dr. H. Buss, whose medical skill may have been better than his poetry, preserved the memory of his visit in verse:

> *Now, Sherman on the Rocky Mountain range,*
> *Eight thousand feet is raised toward the sky,*
> *Indian, Chinese, and many people strange,*
> *Are met or passed as o'er the earth you fly.*

After lunch at Laramie, where "the people around the station are more intelligent-looking than at any place since leaving Omaha," the train was soon across Medicine Bow River and into Carbon Station. Coal had been discovered there and was rapidly replacing wood for fuel on the Union Pacific locomotives. Westbound travelers usually crossed Wyoming's deserts after nightfall, but even by moonlight the endless sweep of dry sagebrush and greasewood was squeezed-lemon appearance," as one observer put it. "There were the usual crumpled dresses, loose hanging and wayward curls, and ringlets, and *possibly* soiled hands and faces; which reduces the fair sex from that state of perfect immaculateness. . . ." Even the self-reliant Susan Coolidge admitted that after two or three days on the Pacific railroad she began to hate herself because she could not contend with the pervasive dust which no amount of brushing or shaking could completely remove from her hair and clothing. And one of the most frequent complaints of all early travelers was the discomfort caused by "the very oppressive smoke" from locomotives which constantly drifted into the cars.

The bracing air of the Sierra, however, was a perfect restorative for the weary travelers. With two locomotives pulling the cars, the train slowly climbed the winding canyon of the Truckee River, rising eighty feet to the mile. Pine and fir replaced the dreary desert sagebrush, and then came a spectacular view of Donner Lake encircled by forested mountains. The guidebooks told the travelers all about the gruesome tragedy of the Donner Party during the winter of 1846–47. And then, as one observer wrote, "after snorting and puffing, whistling and screaming, for an hour and a quarter, our pair of Iron Horses stop in the snow-sheds at the station called 'Summit.' Here we have a good breakfast, well cooked and fairly served; although we could not expect waiters enough to attend in a rush such as they have when the passengers, with appetites sharpened by mountain-air and a long ride, seat themselves at table, and all with one voice cry, 'Steak! coffee! bread! trout! waiter! a napkin!'"

From the summit of the Sierra to Sacramento was 105 miles, a drop from 7,017 feet to thirty feet above sea level. According to William Humason, fifty miles of the descent was made without the aid of steam. "The conductor and brakeman ran the train with brakes on most of the way." For some travelers the ride down the western slope of the range was terrifying, and the coasting trains made so little noise that unwary railroad workers, especially in the snow-sheds, were often struck and killed. "The velocity with which the train rushed down this incline, and the suddenness with which it wheeled around the curves," said William Rae, "produced a sensation which cannot be reproduced in words. . . . The axle boxes smoked with the friction, and the odour of burning wood pervaded the cars. The wheels were nearly red hot. In the darkness of the night they resembled discs of flame."

Corresponding somewhat to the biggest drop and swing of a modern amusement park's roller coaster was Cape Horn, nine miles below Dutch Flat. The guidebooks warned timid passengers not to look down upon the awful gorge of the American River two thousand feet below, and John Beadle said that although Cape Horn offered the finest view in the Sierra, the sight was not good for nervous people. "We're nearing Cape Horn!" someone would always cry out, and the next moment the train would careen around a sharp curve. "We follow the track around the sides of high mountains," said William Humason, "looking down into a canyon of awful depth, winding around for miles, until we almost meet the track we have before been over—so near that one would think we could almost throw a stone across. We have been around the head of the canyon, and have, therefore, 'doubled Cape Horn.'"

Almost as fascinating as the scenery and the roller-coaster ride were the Sierra snowsheds built by engineer Arthur Brown. When passenger service began, these sheds—built with sharp sloping roofs against the mountainsides so that deep snowfalls and avalanches would slide right off them—covered forty miles of track between Truckee and Cape Horn. After numerous passengers complained that the walls blocked their view of the magnificent mountains, the Central Pacific responded by cutting windows at the level of those of the passenger cars. The result was a series of flickering scenes somewhat like those of an early motion picture, but even this pleasure was denied Sierra travelers during the snowy months of winter when the openings had to be closed again.

"A blarsted long depot—longest I ever saw," was the comment of an oft-quoted anonymous Englishman as he passed through the snowsheds, and another British traveler said he had never seen "a more convenient arrangement for a long bonfire. The chimney of every engine goes fizzing through it like a squib, and the woodwork is as dry as a bone." To prevent fires the Central Pacific kept watchmen at regular intervals inside the sheds, with water barrels and hand pumps always ready to extinguish blazes set by

Passengers were endlessly diverted by prairie-dog villages, and sometimes they bought the animals from local boys to take home as pets.
BOTH: *Frank Leslie's Illustrated Newspaper*

sparks from locomotives. There was little they could do, however, against the forest fires which sometimes swept across sections of sheds. And sturdy though the structures were, an occasional mighty avalanche would crush one of them. The train on which Lady Hardy was traveling was delayed all night by the collapse of a shed while fifty male volunteers from among the passengers went ahead to clear the tracks.

The snowsheds not only covered the main track, they also enclosed stations, switch tracks, turntables, and houses where workmen lived with their families. Children were born in this eerie, dimly lit world where without warning a huge boulder or avalanche might crash through the roof, where trains derailed with disastrous results, and at least on one occasion wild animals escaped from a wrecked circus train to terrify the inhabitants. As snowplows were improved, some sheds were removed, others were replaced with concrete, and the army of workmen declined to a handful of lookouts and track walkers.

Although passage through the Sierra was their introduction to California, most westbound travelers did not feel that they had truly reached that golden land until their

Sacramento was almost the end of the line; the Rockies and the plains were behind the passengers, and they had only eighty-odd miles left to go before they reached San Francisco. William Hahn painted this fine view of a busy day at the Sacramento railroad station in 1874.

iron horse brought them down into the blazing sunshine and balmy air of the Sacramento Valley and the flowers and orchards of the Queen City of the Plain. "We seem in a new world," said one. "The transition was sudden and the transformation magical," said another. "The sun descended in a flood of glory toward the Pacific Ocean." In Sacramento they were still more than a hundred miles from the Pacific, and like inspired pilgrims most decided to travel on to that legendary Western sea. Until 1870 they transferred to the cars of the California Pacific, which took them to Vallejo—where again they had to change, this

time to a steamboat running down the bay to San Francisco. After the Central Pacific completed its subsidiary Western Pacific to Oakland in 1870, the journey was easier, although they still made the final crossing by boat before reaching San Francisco and the Pacific shore. After a week of noise, dust, and locomotive smoke the first act of those travelers who could afford it was to register at the magnificent Palace Hotel and seek out a quiet room and a warm bath.

And what were the feelings of travelers after they had completed their first journey by rail across the American continent? Those from other countries were impressed by the grandeur of the Western land, and of course they made comparisons with their own nations, sometimes favorable, sometimes unfavorable. They found travel by train across the West less tedious because they could walk about in the cars and stand on the platforms to enjoy the passing landscapes, yet at the same time they complained of the lack of privacy. They praised the comforts of the Pullman cars, but deplored the necessity for constantly changing trains. They confessed that before the journey they had feared the rumored American defiance of rules and regulations and recklessness in regard to speed, but they were pleased to find that American railway men held human life in as high regard as it was held in their native lands.

American travelers on the other hand were more concerned with feelings of national pride. After crossing the vastness of the American West, the endless unclaimed fertile lands, the prairies and forests, the broad rivers and towering mountains, they felt that they had seen a new map unrolled, a new empire revealed, a new civilization in process of creation. In the first years after the Civil War, the salvation of the Union was still a glorious promise of destiny. "I felt patriotically proud," wrote one traveler to California. He saw the transcontinental railroad as a force binding the Union together "by links of iron that can never be broken." Although Americans were aware that private corporations had built this first railroad to the Pacific, they rejoiced in the belief that California was a rich prize of empire which had been won for them by those connecting links of iron. In their first flush of triumphant pride, they viewed the railroad as a cooperative venture shared by the builders and the people. The disillusionment would come later, as would their doubts in an ever-expanding empire.

For Americans and foreigners alike, there was a deepening sense of wonder at this final link in the encirclement of the earth by steam power. From San Francisco they could now journey to China and Suez by steam-powered vessels, from Suez to Alexandria by rail, from Alexandria to France by water, from France to Liverpool by rail and water, from Liverpool to New York by water, and from New York to San Francisco by rail. In reaching the Western sea, the iron horse had shrunk the planet.

This article has been adapted from Hear That Lonesome Whistle Blow, *the author's eighteenth book on Western history, which will be published later this spring by Holt, Rinehart and Winston.*

Mr. Speaker: The first among the few great representatives who have held the office was Henry Clay. This daguerreotype of the self-confident Kentuckian was taken by Mathew Brady about 1845.

by Neil MacNeil

"The House

In December, 1847, after Robert C. Winthrop of Massachusetts had won election as Speaker of the House of Representatives, three of the nation's most remarkable political leaders stopped by to offer advice. Winthrop, a graduate of Harvard College and scion of one of the country's most distinguished families, was already a veteran of several Congresses and hardly the kind of man who would seek advice. The office he now held, however, was of immense importance. On him, in part, rested the fate of representative government in the United States.

John Quincy Adams told him: "The Speaker of the House of Representatives is next to the President and the Vice President: call upon no one else." Henry Clay advised: "Decide promptly and never give the reasons for your decisions; the House will sustain your decisions, but there will always be men to cavil and quarrel over your reasons." Thomas Hart Benton, a great parliamentarian in his own right, took a third approach: "Be as modest as you please, but don't compromise the House of Representatives."

In these different ways, each laid home to Winthrop the need to protect the power and the dignity of his office, for as Speaker, Winthrop had far more to do than merely preside over the deliberations of the House and sign each engrossed bill passed by the Congress. He had charge of the House of Representatives. He directed its officers and many committees. Not only did he have to keep the boisterous place in order and rule on all procedural questions, but he had above all to see that the House did its work, that it enacted all the bills needed to keep the government functioning.

Winthrop had been chosen Speaker on the third ballot of a spirited contest, the first action taken by that new House of Representatives, then convening for the first time. For every new Congress, the election of a Speaker has always been the first order of business. This is no idle

shall chuse their Speaker..."

And in doing so, the fate of Congress—will it be weak? will it be strong?—is determined

matter: the House cannot function until the Speaker is chosen, nor can the Congress, nor for that matter can the United States government. Once, in the winter of 1855–56, the federal government was all but paralyzed for two months while the House cast no fewer than 133 ballots before electing a Speaker.

Not surprisingly, the House conducts these elections with a litany of rituals almost as old as the republic. In party caucuses, the members-elect choose candidates for the post. When the House meets, with the Clerk of the previous House in the chair temporarily, these candidates are formally nominated, and then the members-elect solemnly vote for one or the other of them. After the results are announced, the loser escorts the winner to the rostrum and graciously introduces him to the cheering spectators. As graciously, the Speaker-elect thanks his colleagues for their show of confidence in him, and pledges to uphold the highest traditions of the House of Representatives to the best of his abilities, and to preside over the deliberations of the House with appropriate fairness. The "Father of the House," its most senior member, then gives the oath of office to the Speaker-elect. That done, the Speaker swears in the other members. Only then is the House ready to do business. Only then does the House formally notify the President that its members are in session and prepared to receive from him whatever communication he may deem fit to send.

The House arrays the election of its Speaker with such solemnities because the members know that the one chosen determines in a real sense the fate of the convening Congress. A weak Speaker forecasts a weak Congress; a strong, dynamic Speaker predicts an energetic, creative Congress. He is "the elect of the elect," the chosen of the people's representatives, and on him more than any other depends the success of the legislative branch.

The post itself is a "constitutional" office, one of the few specified by the Founding Fathers, the "assembly of demi-gods"—as Thomas Jefferson described them—who drafted the Constitution. The members of Congress have always revered the office. In the very first Congress, they voted to pay the Speaker $12 a day, twice the amount they voted for themselves. In the early years, rooms in boarding houses at the capital city were scarce and representatives and senators had to double up, but the Speaker had a room of his own.

Surprisingly, the Founders forgot to set any qualifications for the job. They merely wrote into the Constitution that "The House of Representatives shall chuse their Speaker and other Officers . . ." and let it go at that. Thus, by constitutional proviso, the Speaker need not be a member of Congress, nor even an American citizen. The members of the House are free to elect anyone, of any age or birth or residence. The President and the Vice President must be natural-born citizens, at least thirty-five years old, but the Speaker, technically and legally, could be a Basque shepherd boy or anyone else. This is one of the few oversights by the Founding Fathers, but despite the options open to them, the members of the House have always elected one of their own.

The very lack of definition of the Speaker's office—the debates at the Philadelphia convention in 1787 suggest the Founders gave the matter little thought—seems to indicate that they really intended the Speaker of the House of Representatives to function much like the Speaker of the British House of Commons. Curiously, that office, which had existed more than five hundred years at the time of the American Constitutional Convention, had had a widely varied history. The first English Speaker seems to have been Peter de Montfort, who presided over what was called "the Mad Parliament" in 1258. (The English

The Czar: Republican Thomas B. Reed wielded his powers cynically. "The minority be d——d" is the title of this Puck *cartoon.*

long have had a charming way of nicknaming their parliaments—"the Rump Parliament," "the Addled Parliament," "the Bad Parliament," "the Barebones Parliament"—that Americans unhappily have not mimicked. With a singular lack of imagination, we tend merely to label a Congress either "rubber-stamp" or "do-nothing.")

The English in the old days played a brand of politics far rougher than any imagined now, and for a century and a half, starting in 1399, a disquietingly large number of their Speakers were brought to trial and beheaded. In this same period, of course, the English Speaker normally was little more than the king's spy in Parliament, and his subservience to the royal house did not endear him to the Commons. All this changed by the seventeenth century, when the Speaker became the spokesman for the House, and its foremost defender. In the most dramatic confrontation in the history of the English Parliament, King Charles I broke into the House of Commons in 1642 with

five hundred heavily armed troops to seize five Members of Parliament he had charged with treason. The king demanded that the Speaker, William Lenthall, tell him where they were hiding. Lenthall fell to his knees and refused: "May it please your Majesty, I have neither eyes to see, nor tongue to speak in this place, but as the House is pleased to direct me, whose servant I am here." The king got none of the five, and a few years later this same Parliament voted to cut off *his* head. It was instructive to future kings, parliaments, and Speakers.

By the eighteenth century, the English Speaker had become the dispassionate, impartial officer that he is today. As early as 1604, the English House instructed its Speaker that although he could explain a pending question he was not to "sway the House with argument or dispute." This was the style of Speaker the Founding Fathers knew, and this was the kind of presiding officer the first American Speakers proved to be: dignified, impartial, judicious fel-

28

lows. Like the British Speakers, the American Speakers were not to harangue the House nor engage in factional politics, and the first American Speaker, Frederick Muhlenberg of Pennsylvania, met that mark: a portly, prosperous mediocrity who made an ideal moderator.

This was not to last. By the late 1790's, partisan politics had engulfed Congress forever, and the House elected Theodore Sedgwick of Massachusetts, as partisan a politician as ever stuffed a ballot box, as its fourth Speaker. The fifth Speaker, Nathaniel Macon of North Carolina, elected in 1801, was the friend and ally of President Jefferson and frankly a party stalwart, as was his successor, Joseph Varnum of Massachusetts, elected Speaker in 1807. Clearly the American Speakers were following their own course, sharply different from their English model. Sedgwick offended the House by joining in debate from the chair, but he did debate; Macon insisted as well on his right to vote on legislation; and Varnum showed a marked inde-

pendence from executive influence. Among them, they suggested the power potential within the office if it fell to an ambitious, talented man, as now it did: Henry Clay of Kentucky.

Clay was thirty-four years old when he first entered the House on November 4, 1811, and he was elected Speaker that very day. The office was never the same again. Over a dozen years, Clay was six times elected Speaker. Tall and graceful, he had an easy familiarity in private, but in public he could assume a grandeur almost unmatched in his time. Unfailingly courteous, he radiated self-assurance. His voice was his great strength, a melodious musical instrument that ranged from the playful to the majestic.

Clay knew that he had a majority of the House at his back and he used it. He was the first to control the substance of legislation by his committee appointments. Under him the House devised the so-called "Previous Question" rule as a means of limiting debate. He had bills to enact and enact them he did. He forced a declaration of war against Great Britain in 1812, and he forced the recognition by this country of the newly independent Latin American republics.

Clay was a skillful leader who beguiled his audiences and his colleagues with charm, wit, and eloquence. It was said of him that he could take snuff more elegantly than any man of his time. When the British were marching on Washington, a proposal was offered that Congress go out to fight the enemy, but Clay stated that he would be sorry to lead such a disorderly body into battle. Once, on leaving a convivial party at dawn, he was asked how he could expect to preside over the House that day. "Come up," he said, "and you will see how I throw the reins over their necks!" More than anyone else, he showed what effect a forceful, dynamic Speaker could have on the House of Representatives: he made it, in his time, the dominant branch of the federal government.

Bold and self-confident, Clay understood the office as essentially political, and as Speaker he took command of the House. He was the first great Speaker, the model for Speakers who came later. Never after his tenure would the office revert to the bland impartiality of Speaker Muhlenberg. Lesser men, many of them, succeeded to the Speakership in the decades after Clay, but it was he who permanently settled the nature of the job. Clay failed in only one ambition. "I would rather be right than be President," he said, but his friends knew he would rather have

Uncle Joe: Tough, wizened Joseph G. Cannon was, like fellow Republican Reed, a legislative tyrant and was also called "Czar."

been President. Curiously, only one Speaker of the House, James K. Polk, ever went on to become President.

Now, a century and a half after Clay left the office, the House can count few Speakers who could match his marvelous command of the place, who could rank with him as one of the greats of the House. There have been some: James G. Blaine of Maine, who restored clear-cut majority rule after decades of splinter-party chaos; John G. Carlisle of Kentucky, who devised a question—"For what purpose does the gentleman rise?"—that gave the Speaker control of the recognizing of members and with it control of the House's agenda; Thomas B. Reed of Maine, who broke forever the ability of the minority to filibuster and thereby frustrate action by the majority.

A huge man physically, Reed had a caustic, cynical view of life and politics. He was careless in his manner and nonchalant in his parliamentary talents, and he concealed his ambitions behind a masklike face. He was a political original, the first Speaker called "Czar."

Sardonic in his wit, glacial in his bearing, it was Reed who gave the House its definition of a statesman: "a successful politician who is dead." (Henry Cabot Lodge asked Reed, "Why don't you die and become a statesman?" Reed replied, "No, fame is the last infirmity of a noble mind.") He scorned the opposition: "The right of the minority is to draw its salaries and its function is to make a quorum." When he decided a question, he would inform the minority leaders: "Gentlemen, we have decided to perpetrate the following outrage." Reed brought to fulfillment the power within the Speakership that Clay had first attempted. He controlled the place so thoroughly that he refused to discuss legislation at the White House: he settled such questions without the guidance or advice of the President.

As powerful as Reed was Joseph G. Cannon of Illinois—"Uncle Joe" to his colleagues. Reed ran the House alone; Cannon worked with a handful of trusted lieutenants, and, like Reed, he too was called "Czar." Cannon, a peppery, partisan scrapper, a wizened sixty-seven years old when he was first elected Speaker, took great pride in his own commonness. "I am," he boasted, "one of the great army of mediocrity which constitutes the majority." He ruled the House with an iron grip, and he could laugh at his own notoriety. "Behold Mr. Cannon, the Beelzebub of Congress!" he once shouted at a crowd. "Gaze on this noble, manly form—me, Beelzebub—me, the Czar!"

Cannon was a genial fellow, personally popular with his colleagues, despite his tyrannical methods, but at last he brought on by those methods a great revolt within the House. It came in 1910, and the Speakership was stripped of the powers accumulated over the decades: the minority's rights were carefully written into the House's new rules.

For a decade and a half afterward, in the hands of Champ Clark of Missouri and then Frederick Gillett of Massachusetts, the Speakership went into eclipse, with the real power in the House resting with the majority party's floor leader. It was Nicholas Longworth of Ohio, floor leader under Speaker Gillett, who restored the real power to the chair when he was elected Speaker in 1925. A talented violinist, the son-in-law of President Theodore Roosevelt, Longworth could not become as powerful as Reed and Cannon had been; the rules now prevented that. He used other means, less harsh, to rebuild the Speaker's flagging powers. One was the so-called "Board of Education," a Capitol hideaway where he and his close friend, the leader of the opposition, John Nance Garner of Texas, poured drinks after hours in prohibition-ridden Washington. "Well, you get a couple of drinks in a young Congressman," Garner explained, "and then you know what he knows and what he can do. We pay the tuition by supplying the liquor." Garner succeeded Longworth as Speaker in 1931, and he continued the "Board of Education" in the old way.

In modern times, the man universally recognized as the great Speaker was Sam Rayburn of Texas—"Mr. Sam," as he was called. He served in the House more than forty-eight years, seventeen of them as Speaker, longer by far than any other. (One Speaker, Theodore Pomeroy of New York, served only a single day, March 3, 1869.) Rayburn used the "Board of Education," as had Longworth and Garner, to keep current with everything going on in Congress. It was there where the White House switchboard found Vice President Harry Truman on the day President Franklin D. Roosevelt died. Rayburn's real power flowed from his personal integrity and his almost intuitive sense of the changing moods of the House. He could tell where the House stood on a question by quietly canvassing the members on the House floor. "You can't really say how you lead," he once said. "You feel your way, receptive to those rolling waves of sentiment, and if a man can't see and hear and feel, why then, of course, he's lost."

Rayburn stood only five feet seven, and he was prematurely bald, but he was an imposing figure all the same. He had a politician's love of good storytelling, although he drew the line on the off-color. He paid special attention to new members of the House, encouraging them to take full part in its proceedings. There was nothing arbitrary about Rayburn, although his anger came quickly if he discovered that a colleague had lied to him. "I don't remember what

I say," he liked to remark; "I don't have to."

Rayburn had to negotiate with his committee chairmen; he could not order them as Reed and Cannon once had done. "If you want to get along," Rayburn would say, "go along." He had to depend on persuasion, on appeals to patriotism, on personal friendships, to get done in the House what he believed needed doing. "If you have common sense," he declared, "you have all the sense there is."

Rayburn's friendships within the House extended to the opposition party, and that was not unique with him. He was once asked to go to Massachusetts to help defeat Joseph Martin, leader of the House opposition. "Speak against Martin!" Rayburn exploded. "Hell, if I lived up there, I'd vote for him!"

Rayburn long held power, and, in his own way, he had examined what was needed for its successful, effective use: "a man with brains in his head and iron in his backbone." He had both, and so did the other great Speakers: Garner and Longworth and Cannon, all of whom he had known, and Reed, Carlisle, Blaine, and Clay.

Rayburn died in 1961, and he was not an easy Speaker to follow. By his long service, by his striking personality, he had come to personify what Reed once said the Speaker should be: "the embodiment of the House, its power and dignity."

In the sixteen years since Rayburn, John McCormack of Massachusetts and Carl Albert have in turn served in his place, and in those years the House of Representatives has changed so much that Rayburn himself would be startled. The majority Democrats have especially reformed their ways. Rayburn was saddled with a rigid seniority system that made committee chairmen independent and uncontrollable; that system has been broken. He confronted a recalcitrant House Rules Committee; that committee now has been tamed and made again an arm of the leadership, as in the days of Reed and Cannon. The party's caucus no longer shrinks from ordering action by House committees; the party's steering committee has new authority to sustain the Speaker, and, in sum, the powers of the Speaker have been restored to a greater degree than at any time since the revolt in 1910 against "Czar" Cannon.

Speaker Albert, especially, played a central role in this long struggle to reform the House and its committees, to return to the Speaker many of the powers long lost. A gentle, somewhat diffident man who disliked disciplining his colleagues, Albert hesitated to use the very powers he helped regain. Indeed, he contented himself with that restoration and then announced his own retirement. Those powers are still there, however, waiting for "a man with brains in his head and iron in his backbone."

Neil MacNeil is a correspondent in the Washington bureau of Time *magazine and is author of* Forge of Democracy *(David McKay Company, 1963), a history of the House of Representatives.*

Mr. Sam: A modern standard was set by Sam Rayburn of Texas, a Speaker of great personal integrity and acute political sense.
WIDE WORLD

THE GREAT BLIZZARD OF '88

by Nat Brandt

At fifty-eight years of age, Roscoe Conkling was still a strapping figure of a man, proud of his strength. The former senator, presidential aspirant, and kingpin of Republican politics in New York State neither smoked nor imbibed. He exercised and boxed regularly. So when William Sulzer, a young lawyer who had an office on the same floor as Conkling's in a Wall Street building, could not find a cab, Conkling decided to leave for his club, two and a half miles away, "on my pins."

The deserted streets outside were clogged with fallen telephone and telegraph poles and blocked, as Sulzer recalled, "by great mountains of snow.... We could hardly see Trinity Church, or the buildings on Broadway." Conkling led the way, telling Sulzer to follow in his footsteps. Struggling against a fierce, bitterly cold wind, the two men reached the Astor House a few blocks away. Sulzer gave up and urged Conkling to join him in seeking refuge inside the hotel. But Conkling refused and continued on his own:

"It was dark, and it was useless to try to pick out a path, so I went magnificently along shouldering drifts.... I was pretty well exhausted when I got to Union Square, and, wiping the snow from my eyes, tried to make out the triangles [pathways that crisscrossed the park] there. But it was impossible. There was no light, and I plunged right through on as straight a line as I could determine upon....

"I had got to the middle of the park and was up to my arms in a drift. I pulled the ice and snow from my eyes and held my hands up there till every-

thing was melted off so that I might see; but it was too dark and the snow too blinding...."

It took Conkling twenty minutes to wrestle free from the huge snowdrift, coming "as near giving right up and sinking down there to die as a man can and not do it. Somehow I got out and made my way along." Covered with snow and ice, he finally reached his club and collapsed inside the lobby. It had taken him three hours to get there. He had fought his way through the worst snowstorm in the history of New York City, the Blizzard of 1888.

There have been snowfalls that were greater, hurricanes with winds that were stronger, cold waves when temperatures plummeted lower, but never a combination of the three that was so devastating. The blizzard caught the entire Northeast by surprise, and for nearly two days isolated the nation's largest metropolis.

Spring had been in the air as the weekend of March 10–11 began. The winter had been the mildest in seventeen years. On Saturday the Barnum, Bailey, and Hutchinson Circus had arrived in New York from its winter headquarters and that night staged a two-mile-long torchlight parade through lower Manhattan. Robins were sighted by bird watchers, trees were budding, crocuses were up. Walt Whitman turned in a poem to the New York *Herald*, where he was staff poet; he called it "The First Dandelion" ("Simple and fresh and fair from winter's close emerging .../The spring's first dandelion shows its trustful face."). The city's major department stores were planning spring sales to begin on Monday. And John J.

Only a few onlookers are on hand to survey the mess left by the storm in what ordinarily was a busy thoroughfare in the heart of Manhattan's financial district—New Street. Wall Street is in the background.

33

New Yorkers plod through a snow-choked street, passing a wagon buried in a drift.
CULVER

Meisinger, buyer and manager of Ridley's department store on Grand Street, was the laughingstock of the city. On Friday Meisinger had purchased for the "ridiculous low price" of $1,200 a carload of unclaimed snow shovels; a *Herald* reporter happened on the story and called it "Meisinger's Folly." The shovels were delivered to Ridley's on Saturday, the warmest day of the year; temperatures were in the fifties.

Thousands of miles apart two major weather fronts were headed toward the Northeast. The first, a winter snowstorm from the West, had been spawned in the Pacific and was now racing across the continent on freezing winds at the rate of six hundred miles a day. At the same time a warm, moist-air front born in the Gulf of Mexico was moving northward from Georgia.

Experts at the meteorological headquarters of the Army Signal Corps in Washington—a forerunner of the modern Weather Bureau—knew about both storm systems: the western snowstorm had already hit Minnesota, and gale winds from the warm front had been recorded in parts of Tennessee, Alabama, and Mississippi. But they believed both systems would either dissipate before nearing the eastern seaboard or else blow themselves out harmlessly at sea.

The Washington office and its substations around the country routinely shut down from 10 o'clock Saturday night until five o'clock Sunday afternoon. Before closing up his office on

the top floor of the Equitable Building on Broadway, Sergeant Elias Dunn, chief of the New York substation, reviewed telegraphed reports from Washington and the latest reports telephoned, telegraphed, or sent by carrier pigeon from observers along the coast. Dunn predicted that Sunday in New York would be "cloudy followed by light rain and clearing." He rechecked his findings with the Coast Guard, telephoned his forecast to night editors at the city's newspapers, and went home.

The "light rain" became a downpour as Sunday dawned. When Dunn returned to work that afternoon it was evident something highly unusual was in the offing. He could not raise Washington on his telegraph.

The outer edges of the two storms converged near Lewes Harbor at the mouth of the Delaware River by Cape Henlopen. The gracefully curved harbor, protected both by its location and a breakwater, was a favored port for coastal vessels. Although Sunday had been a gloomy day, the barometer remained high until afternoon, when the first vessels began to seek the harbor's shelter from rapidly increasing winds. A heavy downpour followed, and then at midnight an eerie calm set in. The wind died down, then shifted to almost the opposite point of the compass, blowing in from the west-northwest, the only unprotected side of the harbor. The velocity of the wind increased steadily, the thermometer fell abruptly, and snow began to fall. "It sounded to me like the noise of distant thunder coming nearer and nearer," a captain said.

Hurricane-like winds and blinding snow struck with incredible fury. Anchors broke, rigging and sails were packed with ice and snow, rudders and tillers froze. Vessels ran aground, collided, foundered, while their crews tried desperately to reach safety. One sailor, lashed to the shrouds, froze to death, while his crewmates waited futilely for rescuers to reach their vessel by lifeboat. A schooner laden with a cargo of ice from Maine ran aground, sprang a leak, and soon was itself a solid mass of ice; pounded by the wind, the vessel was knocked to pieces. Two other vessels were driven from their anchors and swept out to sea. One, a coal barge, disappeared entirely; of the other, a bark, only spars, timbers, and cabins were later sighted. Thirty-five of the fifty vessels in the harbor were

destroyed; three bodies were washed ashore.

In New York the rain changed to snow shortly after midnight, the temperature fell rapidly, the wind rose sharply. By six o'clock Monday morning, March 12, as the first city residents were preparing to go to work, the thermometer stood at 23 degrees and was still falling; winds averaged thirty-six miles an hour, with gusts as high as eighty-four miles an hour. Driven by the fierce winds, the snow in freakish fashion piled up on one side of some streets, leaving only a slick coating on the other. As the day wore on, the temperature dropped to five above zero, and winds climbed to an average of forty-eight miles an hour—and no respite was in sight.

At the height of the storm in mid-afternoon, the anemometer perched twenty-five feet above the Equitable Building's east tower broke. One of Sergeant Dunn's assistants, meteorologist Francis Long—a veteran Arctic explorer and survivor of one expedition that had been trapped for three years near the North Pole—offered to repair it. Dunn demurred at first; Long was a heavy man, and the anemometer had just clocked the wind at seventy-five miles an hour. But Long insisted. As Dunn and several other aides braced the thin pole, Long shinnied up it to the top and fixed the instrument, thus enabling the weather station, said Dunn, to preserve "the principal record" of the storm.

What seems amazing is that anyone even contemplated going to work that morning. But in a time before "workers' benefits" and "job security," clerks and laborers were afraid to lose a day's pay. Bankers and stockbrokers were worried about notes and loans due; shopkeepers felt obliged to open their doors for their employees—and besides, most people did not realize the extent of the storm. If they could get out of their homes, they headed for work. For all—rich and poor, young and old—it was a new experience. A blizzard, after all, was common enough in the West, but a phenomenon of such proportions had not struck the Northeast before.

"It was as if New York had been a

Fierce winds force one man to hold fast to a lamppost while another vainly strives to rescue his umbrella. The scene is Twenty-sixth Street at the height of the blizzard.
BETTMANN ARCHIVE

34

burning candle upon which nature had clapped a snuffer, leaving nothing of the city's activity but a struggling ember," the New York *Evening Sun* declared. ". . . The city's surface was like a wreck-strewn battlefield." Of the fifteen mail trains due in New York that Monday morning, only four had arrived by 12:55 P.M., when the city became, for all intents and purposes, cut off from the outside world. All the clocks that ran by electricity in Manhattan had stopped at precisely 12:07 P.M. when the regulator wire broke. Phone and telegraph wires were, like the mass-transit services, aboveground. The wires became coated with ice, poles broke, lines got entangled. Surveying the wreckage, a phone official found 150 poles down on Tenth Avenue, as many fallen on two other West Side streets, and dozens more in other blocks.

One by one the city's four elevated railroads slowed to a halt, their tracks too slippery with ice to provide traction. One train on the Sixth Avenue El took six hours and twenty-five minutes to cover only two blocks. At the height of what was normally the morning rush hour a Third Avenue El train, drawn by a small locomotive called a "dinkie" and pushed by another in back, rammed into a stalled train at the upgrade just outside the Seventy-sixth Street stop; an engineer was killed and fourteen people injured. Thousands of passengers were stranded high above the streets. Enterprising men ran up ladders to the cars and charged the passengers as much as two dollars apiece to climb down.

Streetcar service closed down as the cars ran off their tracks, or the horses could not make any headway. The cars were abandoned where they stood. Walter Hall, a driver on a line that ran from Ninety-ninth Street to the Bowery, gave up just short of his destination. He ordered his passengers out, sent his horses off to a stable with a boy, and found some coal in the neighborhood to stoke his little stove. When two men with a keg asked for shelter inside the car, Hall took them in and the three stayed in the car for three days, "living," said Hall, "on beer and pretzels."

Commuter service from the suburbs also broke down early. Samuel M. Davis, telegraph operator for the New York Central & Hudson River Railroad at Spuyten Duyvil, just north of Manhattan, was on duty when the 6:40 Croton local reached the Spuyten

Duyvil Cut, 150 feet deep and five hundred feet long. The train ran smack into a thirty-foot-high snowdrift and could not move forward or backward. Two minutes later the Peekskill local chugged to a halt behind it, then two trains from the West. Within two hours seven trains were strung out behind the Croton local. There were two butcher and grocery shops in town, and Davis "bought everything they had that was eatable— bread, sugar, flour, milk, cured hams, bologna and all the sandwich stuff they had." For the next two days, Davis, his wife, and his mother baked bread and made sandwiches and coffee that they lugged up to the passengers aboard the stalled trains.

New York was the focus of the blizzard, but for a radius of a hundred miles around it—at sea, upstate, in New Jersey, Pennsylvania, and parts of New England—similar conditions prevailed.

In Westchester County, nearly five thousand passengers sought shelter at the Mount Vernon station when forty trains, commuter and long distance, were trapped by snowdrifts. To the south, between the northern end of the Central's tunnel at Ninety-sixth Street and Harlem Junction, six more trains were stalled. Grand Central Terminal itself, as one reporter noted, "looked lonely." In the yards behind it "long lines of passenger cars were stretched throughout its length, but they looked desolate. . . . The snow had blown into the great covered area and gave a chilling and forbidding air to the place." Asked whether the New York Central would be able to maintain any service, Chauncey M. Depew, its president, groaned: "Trains! Why we don't even know whether we've got a railroad left!"

Other railroad lines suffered the same fate, and the number of wrecks was appalling. The Central's Chicago express had been rammed from behind at Dobbs Ferry by another express, the cars telescoping; fortunately, no one was killed. But three people died when a Pennsylvania Railroad train hit a freight that had jumped its track near Huntingdon, Pennsylvania, and blocked all traffic east and west. A Jersey Central local, running "wildcat" without orders from station to station, picking up commuters bound for New York, ran into the rear of a stalled train. Later, a Jersey Central snowplow trying to

push through a drift collided with a snowbound train; three people were killed and six others injured. A Lehigh Valley Railroad brakeman was never seen again after he headed out into the storm to flag down a train.

The greatest losses were suffered at sea; nearly two hundred ships were wrecked or disappeared. Nine of New York's pilot boats foundered in the harbor or lower bay. Another, the *Starbuck*, cruising off the coast waiting to guide ships into port, her running lights veiled by heavy mist, was hit by the British steamer *Japanese* off Barnegat, New Jersey, when winds of a hundred miles an hour tossed the *Japanese* out of control. Five of the *Starbuck*'s crew were lost.

Typical was the experience of the three-masted schooner *R. H. Heniman*, bound for New York from the tropics for provisions before heading up Long Island Sound to Boston. Unable to maneuver in the wind, the *Heniman* made for New London, Connecticut, and had its lighthouse in sight, but was forced out to sea. "The Captain ordered us to abandon our quarters forward and to move into the cabin," one of the seamen recalled. "For three days it snowed. As it grew colder and colder, we could not stick it out on deck more than an hour at a time. One could hardly face the wind as it cut like a knife. We wore all the clothes we could put on. It was necessary to lash the wheel fast and to keep only one man on deck at the time as a lookout for other vessels which might run us down. As our good little vessel plunged and rolled around, a large comber stove a hole in our lifeboat, bending one of the heavy iron davits on which the boat hangs across the stern. We had to cut the boat adrift with everything in her. When abreast of New London we were in company with 12 to 15 schooners bound eastward. Of them all we were one of the few that reached harbor safely. . . ."

Among the ships that did get through was one carrying immigrants from Lithuania. When a passenger named H. N. Davidsohn emerged into the storm, he assumed that this was the normal climate of the area, and sourly concluded that he might just as well have emigrated to Siberia.

As the day wore on it became clear that travel in the city itself was next to impossible. The Wall Street Exchange closed down when only thirty members showed up and only 15,400 shares had been traded by 12:30; more than 360,000 shares had changed hands the previous Monday. At the city's seventy banks, only a small fraction of the $63 million in normal daily deposits was received. As a result cashiers refused to certify checks but, in what was believed an unprecedented action, extended all outstanding loans. Without judges and jury members, the courts closed down. The city prison, the Tombs, was filled to overflowing with men and women who had committed themselves as vagrants; the prison clerk offered to free everyone, but "they all declined with thanks." At City Hall, Mayor Abram Hewitt sent word that there would be no daily conference of department heads; it was an unnecessary gesture—none had appeared anyway.

The fashionable midtown department stores fared poorly. Only one customer showed up at B. Altman & Company all day; she bought a spool of thread. Macy's closed down at noon, but its female clerks were afraid to venture home in the blizzard, so Macy executives let them sleep on cots in the furniture department.

Those that did venture out found walking difficult. "There was a fierce cyclonic wind prevailing as we made our way uptown," said Arthur B. Goodkind, who with three friends had decided to head home, "but good cheer and humor kept us going nicely until we reached 86th Street. At this point, one of the wider streets in the then uptown part of the city, we encountered our greatest difficulty. A goodly number of people were standing on the corner, trying to cross over, but the gale-like wind pushed them back at every attempt. A bright idea occurred to someone who had witnessed marching prisoners. He advised that we form in single line, each man with his hands on the shoul-

The Fastest Commuter in the East

The travails of getting to work during the blizzard were so severe that the New York *Evening Sun gave front-page space to the remarkable story of a businessman who managed to make the trip from then fashionable Harlem to the City Hall area in only two hours and eleven minutes—"probably the fastest time on record for the day." Despite the speed, the trip was not altogether without incident, as the man's account demonstrates:*

I left my house on 128th street and Sixth avenue at 9½ A.M. and at once discovered that it was snowing. I opened my umbrella, and a howling wind swept around the corner from Sixth avenue and took that umbrella out of my hand and lifted it over the roof of a neighboring flat house. Next my Derby hat flew off my head and went skimming over the snow drifts at the rate of about sixty miles an hour. I let it go, returned to my house, put on an old hunting cap, tied up my ears in a woollen muffler, and started out again to go to my business. . . .

I had to get down town, and I went to a livery stable to get a conveyance. There was one cutter, one horse, and one driver left. I hired all three for $15 and started out. That was at 10:20 o'clock. The driver told me that the horse was liable to run away if he got excited, but he didn't get excited. Well, we started down Third avenue on a fast trot, and then the fun began. The air was so full of little fine needles of snow and the wind tore by us at such a rate that that horse staggered about like a drunken man. But he was game. He put his head down and trotted ahead in the teeth of the blast. His mane and tail were masses of ice, and his hide was thickly veneered with it. You know I wear eyeglasses. Well, my eyeglasses were covered with ice so thick that I had to lick it off every five minutes. I couldn't get them clear any other way.

We passed Third avenue surface cars all the way down. They were all deserted and most of them were off the track. The horses had all been taken back to the stables. The brewers' wagons were out, though, out in force, and each one had from four to ten great Normandy horses. Even the great strength of these huge draught animals was not enough to pull the wagons through some of the snow drifts, and the drivers were lashing the poor beasts with their whips and cursing them with great vigor. The sidewalks were almost deserted as well as I could see through my ice-covered glasses. As we kept moving southward at the great speed of four miles an hour, the sleet striking my face made me feel as if it was raining carpet tacks. My moustache froze solid, my eyebrows did likewise, and little icicles formed on my eyelashes and got into my eyes. They hurt like hot cinders.

At Eighty-fourth street I got out, went into a dry goods store, and bought two toboggan caps for the driver and myself. We pulled them down over our ears and tied mufflers over our faces, leaving only the eyes exposed. Then things were more pleasant. The driver was 61 years old, but he didn't grumble a bit.

"I'm an old New York tough," he said. "I've lived here, man and boy, all my life, but I'll be _____ if ever I seen the likes o' this ride, an' I doan' wanter."

And still that good horse went staggering ahead. We tilted nearly over several times and twice we ran into pillars of the elevated road, for we couldn't see where we were going half the time. . . . At Ninth street the fury of the wind redoubled, and when we got to Park row the horse was forced to stagger a little more slowly.

I arrived opposite THE SUN office at 12:31 o'clock, having made the trip in a little more than two hours, and I don't believe anybody beat it. . . . One of the driver's fingers was frozen, and the horse was completely exhausted. No, I am not going home to-night. I have telegraphed to expect me in May.

Typical blizzard vignettes: At top, the wreck of a commuter train at Coleman's Station in Dutchess County, New York. Below that is an artist's depiction of the ice bridge in the East River that enabled people to cross between Manhattan and Brooklyn. At bottom, an abandoned streetcar in the Bowery.

ders of the man ahead, so that those who once had crossed might drag the others along. It was in this fashion only that we were able to do what in other conditions would seem to be the absurdly simple business of crossing a city street."

Those who dared to brave the blizzard wore a strange assortment of clothes—blankets draped from their heads, huge rubber boots, trouser legs tied around their ankles, carpeting bundled over their feet. One youth got some straw wine-bottle covers from a restaurant and bound his feet in them. Another was able to purchase a striped bathrobe and wore it home as an overcoat.

Stores that stocked cold-weather gear sold out quickly. After selling the forty-five dozen pairs of gloves he had put aside for the following winter, one Broadway shopkeeper ingeniously cut apart ten dozen suits of woolen underwear. Each leg was tied with a string at one end and then sold as a pullover cap. The shopkeeper moaned that he had only ten dozen ear muffs on hand: "they were gone as quickly as snow on a summer's day," he said.

Cabbies were getting unheard-of fees for trying to make their way through streets clogged with abandoned wagons, streetcars, and dead horses. And saloons, noted a *Herald* reporter, were "running under full head." "Whiskey has the call," an East Side barkeep said. "The next most popular drink to-day is hot rum." Those in the know, however, stuck to the "car driver's drink"—ale with red pepper; it was supposed to make you warmer faster and last longer.

Everywhere, it seemed, strangers were helping each other out. It was not unusual to find people rubbing each other's ears to thaw them out. And the number of rescues was amazing. A *World* reporter happened to be on Sixth Avenue when he saw a young woman fall unconscious into a snowbank; he carried her into a nearby drugstore where she revived. A police officer spied a butcher's cart near Eighth Street and Second Avenue, its horse collapsing from exhaustion. In the seat was the driver, leaning forward, his head on the dashboard, the reins slipping from his hands. The policeman rubbed the driver's face with snow and with the help of a passer-by got him to walk until he was fully conscious. The driver woke up surprised; he thought he had been at home asleep, safe and sound.

A poorly clad fourteen-year-old messenger boy was found by a porter, crying and exhausted on Thirty-fourth Street, his trousers frozen to his flesh. A university student was trying to find an open grocery store on Third Avenue when he noticed a bundle of clothing in a snowbank; it was a little girl whose father had given her a basket and sent her out to beg. Father Daniel C. Cunnion of the Church of St. Raphael on West Fortieth Street was on a sick call when he saw a hand jutting from the snow; it turned out to be one of his Sunday-school children who had been sent out to get some food.

Others were not so lucky. The old woman who sold flowers in front of the *Herald* offices dropped dead from exposure. A woman in her fifties was found unconscious at Fulton Street and Broadway; she was carried into a liquor store and died ten minutes later. A two-hundred-pound malt-and-hops merchant who suffered from chronic asthma tried to walk to his office from Fifty-seventh Street; a few blocks on he fell into a snowdrift, his weight pulling the snow over him, and was dead when discovered several hours later by two patrolmen. Later, a medical student working at the *Star* to help pay his tuition volunteered to try to reach Coney Island to check out rumors that its famed Brighton Beach Hotel had been swept out to sea; he was able to hitch a ride on a transit-line snowplow, found the hotel intact, and then hired a horse and sleigh for the return trip. He was found unconscious in the snow, his nose, ears, and feet frostbitten; he died before the week was out.

Nancy Sankey-Jones remembered seeing a man try for an hour and a half to cross Ninety-sixth Street. "We watched him start, get $\frac{1}{4}$ way across and then flung back against the building on the corner. The last time he tried it, he was caught up on a whirl of snow and disappeared from our view. The next morning 7 horses, policemen, and his brother charged the drift and his body was *kicked* out of the drift. . . ."

Hundreds of horses perished, too, as well as enormous numbers of sparrows. The sparrows were the city's bane—hundreds of thousands of them nested on trees and on building ledges throughout Manhattan—and they died in the storm, beating their wings helplessly against windows and jam-

ming ventilator shafts trying to seek shelter. Some were eaten by hungry people, for shop supplies dwindled rapidly and the fear of shortages of milk, bread, and meat spread throughout the city. Prices for food boomed— eggs going for forty cents each, the poorest beefsteak for thirty cents a pound, butter for sixty cents.

Fortunately for the more than four hundred children and nearly two hundred mothers at the New York Infant Asylum, a supplier had made an error shortly before the blizzard. Instead of delivering a consignment of twelve dozen cans of condensed milk, he had left off twelve gross. The condensed milk was mixed with barley water and "greatly to our surprise," said the resident physician, Dr. Charles G. Kerley, "the marasmic and difficult

NEW-YORK HISTORICAL SOCIETY

feeders, struggling along on diluted sterilized milk, took on new life, began to smile and gain in weight."

With outside sources cut off, a shortage of coal also became a widespread fear. Augustus E. Cron, a nineteen-year-old deliveryman for a West Eighth Street grocer, recalled how his employer had the good fortune to have ten tons of coal on hand. Men came from all over, begging for coal, "some men with silk hats on even, and gladly paid as much as a dollar a pailful." Cron made deliveries, too, working until midnight, but four times he had to cut the buttons off the coats he wore because the buttonholes were frozen stiff.

More immediate than the danger of starving or freezing to death was the possibility of uncontrollable fires. With several hundred alarm boxes out of order, fire department headquarters ordered all engine houses to

have four horses ready to hitch to steamers and two to hose carts at all times. In many places, piles of snow insulated hydrants and kept the water lines from freezing, but maneuvering through the choked streets was another matter. Answering a summons, one hook-and-ladder company got stuck in a huge snowbank at Twenty-third Street and Eighth Avenue, and even the harnessing of six horses to the wagon failed to budge it.

The concern over fires seemed confirmed when a major one broke out in an old four-story building on Laight Street that housed a paper-box factory and was adjacent to tenements inhabited by immigrants. Streams of water pumped at the building froze on contact with the walls and never reached inside. A waitress at the Old Hygienic Hotel & Turkish Bath across the street recalled:

"We were serving dinner to patrons and many strangers. The place was packed as many people could not get home. When someone cried fire we looked out and sure enough there it was. The fire engine had an awful time getting around. . . . Ice everywhere, water was taken from the swimming pool. When the firemen got the fire plug working there were rivers of water in rooms, hall, and down the stairs. All the windows on the lane side were broken from the heat and as the men came down from the roof their clothes were solid ice. We weighed their hats at 20 lbs. apiece. We tried to give them hot coffee but had to thaw out the mustaches of those who had them. . . ." By a stroke of fortune, no one was injured in the blaze.

As night approached, the city became wrapped in almost complete darkness. The Metropolitan Telephone Company—which had sixty-nine hundred subscribers in Manhattan, mostly businesses—had asked the electric companies not to start up their dynamos at night because their cables were so entangled with the less-insulated phone wires. "These broken telephone wires would have carried the sparks in all directions into awnings, houses, stores and everywhere else," a spokesman told a *Tribune* reporter, "and the effect would have been terrible." Few gas lamps were working either. Only the lights from the windows of houses and saloons— or the little red lamps marking fire plugs—shed any glow on the snow-clogged streets; the effect was eerie.

All the city's hotels were packed. Doubling and tripling up of strangers was common. At the fashionable Astor House, two hundred cots were put in the parlor, halls, and even bathrooms —"the last-named apartments," noted the *Herald*, "being quickly taken by the late arrivals . . . even standing room was at a premium in the evening." Many businesses had the foresight early in the day to reserve rooms for their employees—the Astor had thirteen clerks from the Chemical Bank in one room, fifteen from the Hanover Bank in another. At Smith & McNell's Hotel, which had 420 rooms, eight hundred people were taken in, a thousand turned away. The chief clerk at the Stevens House confided that he had felt "compelled" to rent out even the chairs.

With all travel halted, even the best hotels, which customarily sent their laundry to New Jersey, discovered that they were running out of clean linens. "Fastidious guests," said the *Times*, "were surprised to be blandly informed by their waiters when they sat down to table that there were no napkins, and still more astonished when they found that one towel had to last for 24 hours at least."

Undaunted by the weather or the difficulty of getting around, a few rabid theatergoers managed to find some entertainment. Five new plays were scheduled to open Monday night; none did. But three theaters did hold performances, and despite the blizzard, P. T. Barnum had insisted on staging both his matinee and evening circus shows at the newly renovated Madison Square Garden. "If only one customer had come, I would have given the complete show," he boomed. "My duty is to the public and nothing shall ever keep me from honoring that duty, except Judgement Day itself." As it was, about a hundred persons attended each of the three-and-a-half-hour performances. The variety show at Tony Pastor's Theater on Fourteenth Street, however, drew only four persons. One of them was Frank J. Pfister of Jersey City Heights. Stranded in the city by the storm, he and two friends bought 25-cent balcony seats for the show. There was one other man in the balcony. At 7:30 Pastor approached the footlights and asked if the four wanted refunds. Pfister called down to "go on with the show." The show went on and, to Pfister's surprise, "all the performers responded to our applause just the

same as if the house was crowded." Afterward, Pastor got out a case of champagne and sandwiches and treated the cast and his four customers to a party.

A block away at the Star Theater, Ellen Terry and Henry Irving played to a similarly sparse house in *Faust*. Of all, the best attendance was at Daly's Theater, at Twenty-eighth Street, where 150 persons turned up to see Ada Rehan in *A Midsummer Night's Dream*. "The weather was a far cry from a midsummer's night," said an observer, "but Ada—ah, glorious Ada—was a dream."

Dawn Tuesday found the storm stalled off Block Island, near the entrance to Long Island Sound. The thermometer read five degrees above zero at 5 A.M., the wind was still howling at fifty miles an hour, and the snow continued to fall, but not as much as on the previous day. Early in the morning an unusual incident occurred when an immense ice floe from the Hudson River floated back up the bay on the rising tide. The floe—six inches thick and covered with two inches of snow—turned at the Battery and slowly headed up the East River, but it was so huge that it got wedged between Brooklyn and Manhattan near the Brooklyn Bridge. The bridge itself had been closed to pedestrians, and the cable cars that ran back and forth over it were then out of service. Soon hundreds of persons were crossing over the ice field instead. Several tugs appeared and finally the field was broken up, with five men left hugging cakes of ice and drifting out to sea. Three were on a piece as large as Washington Square, two on cakes no larger than a door mat. The tugs rescued all of them.

Gradually, the city struggled back to life. It warmed up a bit as the day progressed—from one degree below zero at 6 A.M. to 23 degrees at 3 P.M.—though winds still averaged forty-five miles an hour. The elevated railroads were able to start up on Tuesday, but street traffic continued to be badly bottled up. Getting rid of the snow was the major problem. Shovels were at a premium; Ridley's department store chalked up a neat 50 per cent profit selling all the shovels that John Meisinger had bought for the store. The street-cleaning department estimated that below Forty-second Street alone there were 23,560,000 cubic yards of snow that had to be re-

moved, that it would take two weeks to do so, and that twelve million cartloads would be required to dump the snow off river piers. The department hired more than seventeen thousand extra men at twenty-five cents an hour to shovel the snow, and tried to rent a thousand carts from merchants and teamsters. It was a laborious process. The clean-up operation began at Fourteenth Street and Broadway, near the department's stables. Two cross streets were cleared first, so the carts could reach the piers. At the same time, homeowners and shopkeepers tried tunneling their way into the street, and when that didn't work, some started bonfires to melt the snow. Youths were making modest fortunes shoveling sidewalks—anywhere from $10 to $25 a house was common.

Communication with the outside world was restored when a clever reporter for the Boston *Globe* found that he could send dispatches between Boston and New York via London by using the Atlantic Cable. Tuesday afternoon the United Press got a wire working between New York and Washington—a distance of 230 miles—by transmitting via Chicago and Pittsburgh, a distance of twenty-five hundred miles.

What amazed even-then blasé New Yorkers was the good humor that pervaded the city. Signs popped up everywhere on snowbanks: "Keep Off the Grass," "This bank is closed indefinitely," "It's yours—if you want it," "Don't pick the flowers," "Make us an offer."

By Wednesday the worst was over. The temperature, only eight degrees at 3 A.M., rose to 29 degrees by noon and the sun came out. The first mail train to reach New York since Monday, a Pennsylvania Railroad train from Philadelphia, arrived, as did the New York Central mail train from the Midwest that had been due Monday. By 6 P.M., when the reading was 37 degrees and still climbing, Sergeant Dunn at the Signal Corps station forecast "fair and increasingly warm weather." It now looked likely that the nearly five hundred dead bodies awaiting burial since the weekend could finally be interred; when funeral homes had run out of space for the corpses, many had been kept on ice.

By Thursday New York was virtually back to normal, though traffic jams continued to plague the city, and patches of snow remained in shaded sites until June. Mayor Hewitt was convinced now, he said, that the blizzard would have "one good effect ... as it shows the necessity for an underground rapid transit railroad and for getting the wires under ground."

Measured in actual inches of snowfall, the blizzard was not impressive—some sixteen inches had fallen on Monday, a little over four more inches on Tuesday. But other statistics were sobering: nearly one hundred persons lost at sea; as many dead in New York or in the region around it; $20 million in property damage in the city alone, and for the people who worked in it, some seven hundred thousand in all, $500,000 lost in wages. And for all of New York's nearly one and a half million residents it had been an unforgettable experience, almost legendary, one to measure other storms by. Until as recently as 1969, when the

few who were left were too old to meet anymore, a group of survivors known as the Blizzard Men of 1888 continued to observe the anniversary of the storm each year with a dinner at which they swapped anecdotes and rehashed the story of that dreadful day.

Oddly enough, during the storm New Yorkers kept referring to it as a Dakota blizzard. "It seems to have originated in Dakota, a Territory which threatens in our unceremonious nomenclature to be known as the 'Blizzard State,'" a *Herald* editorial declared. "We may do Dakota injustice, which would be unfortunate on the eve of her admission into the family of States, but in the matter of storms she certainly comes off with a bad reputation."

It was meant jokingly, of course, and Dakotans replied in kind. Typical was one of the several telegrams that

were addressed to Mayor Hewitt:

"Huron, Dak., under a mild spring sun, sends her sympathy to blizzard-stricken New York. If need you may draw on us for $50 to relieve the storm sufferers."

Roscoe Conkling, whose trek to the safety of his club had received wide coverage in the nation's press, also got a telegram, from the office of the Fargo *Argus:*

"The Dakota robins, sitting on orange trees, in blossom, join in thanks for your safe delivery from New-York's snowdrifts ... all join with me in congratulations to you and say: 'Come to the banana belt, where every man is your well-wisher.'"

Whether Conkling enjoyed the jest is not known. He died early in the morning of April 18 of otitis media and suppurative inflammation of the mastoid cells with pulmonary edema—the last victim of the blizzard. ☆

The aftermath of the blizzard: Pedestrians make their way down a partly cleared sidewalk beside one of the city's El lines.
CULVER

41

Say, who's that tall, homely feller in the stovepipe hat?

CULVER

Why, that's George Billings.

George Billings? Certainly, in Al and Ray Rockett's long-forgotten silent epic *Abraham Lincoln* in 1924. The gaunt, familiar form of Lincoln has been a stock dramatic figure ever since May of 1861, when a political potboiler called *Abe's Saturday; or Washington Sixty Days Hence* opened at Boston's Mobile Theater.

No one seems to know how many times Lincoln has appeared on stage or screen over the intervening years. No one has counted how many rails he has split, or tears he has shed over Ann Rutledge; how many times he has said good-by to Springfield, or freed the slaves, or just waited, docile, for John Wilkes Booth to slip up behind him. The number must be staggering.

Distinguished writers like John Drinkwater, Robert E. Sherwood, and James Agee have mounted full-scale dramatic lives of Lincoln. But more often he has been used as a sentimental walk-on—letting Shirley Temple perch on his lap, perhaps, as he did in *The Littlest Rebel* (1935), or admonishing Jimmy Stewart to write to his worried mother in *Of Human Hearts* (1938).

On the facing page are six actors who have played Lincoln over the last century, plus one genuine portrait of the great man himself. Can you tell which one it is, as well as who's who beneath the grease paint? Answers appear below.

(A) Dennis Weaver in *The Great Man's Whiskers*, a 1973 TV production   (B) Hal Holbrook in the 1976 TV series *Sandburg's Lincoln*   (C) Walter Huston in D. W. Griffith's *Abraham Lincoln*, 1930   (D) Lincoln himself, photographed in 1863   (E) Raymond Massey leaves for Washington in Robert Sherwood's play, *Abe Lincoln in Illinois*, 1939   (F) John Carradine in the film *Of Human Hearts*, 1938   (G) Frank McGlynn in John Drinkwater's play, *Abraham Lincoln*. 1919

A

B

C

D

E

F

G

43

THE INSPIRED LEAK

by Bruce Catton

ILLUSTRATION BY RICHARD AND MARK HESS

The leak was known of old. It can afflict either a ship or a government, it invariably means that something invisible has gone wrong, and in certain cases it ends in disaster. It is instructive to reflect on the differences between the leak as known to mariners and the leak as known to politicians, political scientists, and newspaper correspondents.

When a ship develops a leak, water that the crew tries to keep out comes in, and if the leak goes on long enough the ship goes down. The case may be ominous, but basically it is simple enough. A defect has developed somewhere in the outer skin, and in most cases it can readily be found and closed.

When a government develops a leak, a truth that the crew tries to keep in comes out, and if this goes on long enough something is assuredly going to founder—a career, a man, or even the government itself. This case may also be ominous, but it usually is not simple at all. A defect has developed far down inside somewhere, sometimes at the very heart of things, and although the leak can often enough be located it may be quite impossible to close it.

This sort of leak afflicts governments in free countries only. In a totalitarian land people know only what they are officially told, and anyone who tries to tell them things unofficially quickly learns that this is not healthful. But in democracies there are few such restrictions, and the leak is a familiar institution—is, in fact, one of the things that make democracy work.

Every government now and then develops information of one kind or another that in the opinion of the men in charge ought to be kept secret; which is to say that the government does something or plans to do something or has just finished doing something that people on the outside are not supposed to know about. In all such cases secrecy is imposed; but the secrecy never works—at least it never works very long—because there are always some government officials who disapprove of the secret that is being protected, or disapprove of the mere act of keeping things secret, or have personal or political antagonism for the secret-keepers, and these dissidents invariably find a way to bring the secrets out into the open. They leak, in other words. Information that is supposed to remain hidden gets into the hands of outsiders, including chiefly the press, and then nature and an aroused citizenry take their course.

In America of recent years this whole business of the official leak has become highly systematized, and on occasion most of the really interesting news in the daily press is the product of leaks. Such stories can be recognized at once by unvarying stigmata. The news is never attributed to any identifiable person, as is the case when some formal announcement or enactment is being reported. Instead the news is said to come from "sources close to" the White House or a cabinet member or a congressional committee, or whatnot. Just to prove that he is not writing something

45

which he himself dreamed up, the writer will often hang every paragraph on a "sources said" limb.

This is the unfailing sign that somebody has been leaking. All that the reader needs to do, by way of caution, is remember that whoever is doing the leaking has reasons of his own for doing it. When you see a "sources said" story you may be sure that an axe is being ground, somewhere down out of sight. It may well be ground in your own interest, of course, but the one certainty is that the leak did not just happen. Somebody has got an angle.

For underneath every leak is the fact that there is a division in the ranks of the government's servants. Somebody in this service wants to prevent, hasten, water down, or intensify what his colleagues or superiors are doing. One cabinet member may oppose the actions of another cabinet member and plant stories about it where they will do the most good. Employees of a President, a department head, a congressional committee, or a government agency wish to stop one action or to promote another, so they reveal secrets to news gatherers; and so the public learns things that it would not otherwise know, which is sometimes all to the good and sometimes is not but which can have a profound effect on what finally happens. And the person who starts all of this is never, in any case, disinterested.

Instances of the power and prevalence of the leak are too numerous in recent history and too vivid in all recent memories to need recalling here. Important policies have been overhauled, changed, or abandoned outright because of leaks; relations with foreign countries have been altered, public men have dropped out of sight, and on one noteworthy occasion an entire administration came to disaster via the "informed sources" route, with rats leaving the ship so fast that even the dullest reader could know that the ship was about to sink.

The fact that the leak has been elevated to one of the most important mechanisms by which the democracy governs itself simply means that the overwhelming power of public opinion is finally being recognized; or, if that power has always been recognized, it is at least being called on to act much earlier than ever before. In the old days public opinion came into play after congressional debates or presidential announcements; now it comes first, applying a final inexorable verdict to actions, programs, and ideas that are still in the formative stage. The process of government has taken on a new velocity and is responsive to a new set of controls. Nobody, including those who have the most immediate access to those controls, really knows what responsibilities are involved or what the ultimate consequences may be. Like so many of the great changes in American life, this one has gone into operation without the benefit of any advance planning whatever. The blithe insouciance with which the new controls are being handled is most engaging and also just a little bit disturbing.

Nothing quite like the modern manipulation of the leak can be found in the past. (The emphasis here, of course, is on the word *quite*. The thing is organized and systematized now in a way the Founding Fathers never could have anticipated.) But ours has always been a democratic government, which means that it has always been somewhat loose-jointed, which in turn means that there have always been leaks. Some of these, like some of today's, have had an important part in the nation's history.

Consider, for instance, the once-famous case of the Ostend Manifesto.

In 1853 a pleasant nonentity from New Hampshire named Franklin Pierce was President of the United States. His administration wanted to annex Cuba—an idea strongly supported by militant spokesmen for the slave states and by fuzzy-minded folk who had a vague belief that America just ought to expand somewhere regardless, but strongly opposed by Northerners who were having increasing doubts about slavery and the people who supported it. Pierce's administration thought it might be possible to persuade Spain to sell Cuba—$130 million tops was what it had in mind—and if this could not be done, which would probably be the case, perhaps somebody could stir up an uprising in Cuba that would detach the island from Spanish dominion. If that happened, annexation by the United States would take place as a matter of course. They hoped.

This was quite an idea, but it was clear that the times were not propitious. Overseas there was the beginning of the Crimean War, which created troubled waters but probably did not create conditions favorable for a New World republic that wanted to fish in them. At home there was the beginning of something that the Pierce administration was bound to consider of paramount importance—the Kansas-Nebraska fight over slavery, stirring up strong-minded men who considered the Cuban program either irrelevant or an abominable crime.

As a makeshift, the administration convened a meeting of three of its most important diplomats—James Buchanan, minister to Great Britain; Pierre Soulé, minister to Spain; and John Mason, minister to France. These men were to meet, compare notes on the attitudes of the governments to which they were accredited, and see what sort of program could be worked out. The meeting was to be held in Paris, but no secrets could be kept in Paris and it was agreed to have the meeting in Ostend. So ordered, for October 9.

The conferees met, meditated on their own importance, and took the bit in their teeth. Drafting a top-secret memorandum for Washington, they proposed that the United States try to buy Cuba outright and that if this failed (as it certainly would, the proud Spaniards being in no mood to sell) the United States should consider whether it ought not to go ahead and take Cuba by force of arms. This went far beyond anything desired by the American Secretary of State, William L. Marcy, for whom all of these ministers worked, but this was what they wanted and anyway the whole business was completely secret.

Except that these men included, in their persons and on their staffs, some of the leading flannelmouths in American history, and garbled versions of what had been proposed immediately appeared in newspapers in Europe and America. There had been, in other words, a wholesale leak, coming not because anyone had an axe to grind but simply because the men involved just could not keep their flapping mouths shut. The Ostend Manifesto, as it became known, raised a storm on both sides of the Atlantic. By March of 1854 Secretary Marcy (who had planned to let the idea simmer quietly for a time) had to send the report to Congress, which made it public property. That killed it. The administration had lost the fall elections, the rising clamor over slavery in Kansas and Nebraska made the addition of more slave territory in the Caribbean unthinkable, and the Ostend Manifesto quickly died, surviving in the national memory only as an oddity for historians. An act of immeasurable folly had been prevented by a leak.

A leak of quite a different kind came three years later. James Buchanan of Pennsylvania, another amiable man, known in the political jargon of the times as a doughface— a northern man with southern principles—had been elected President of the United States and was to take office on March 4, 1857. The nation just then was wracked by the question of Popular Sovereignty—the notion that the people of a territory should decide for themselves, before statehood, whether in that territory slavery should be permitted or excluded. Stephen Douglas of Illinois, proprietor of the northern half of the Democratic Party, had staked his political future on the idea that the people of a territory should have that right; the party's southern wing, with which Buchanan was intimately allied, was firm in the faith that such a right did not and under the Constitution should not exist. Buchanan was about to deliver an inaugural address in which he was bound to declare himself on this issue, and he was painfully aware that no matter which side he took he would alienate—probably forever, because tempers were inflamed—half of the party that had elected him. A politician who believed in offending nobody could not face a more dreadful situation.

However, he saw a glimmer of hope. The Supreme Court was about to hand down a decision in the case of Dred Scott, and there was a fair chance that this might take Buchanan off the hook—if he could just know in advance which way the cat was going to jump.

Dred Scott was a black slave, originally owned by an army officer in St. Louis. This officer presently was transferred to duty in Rock Island, Illinois, and later to Fort Snelling, Minnesota. He took Scott with him, and when at last he was ordered back to St. Louis he took Scott along; and now Scott was suing for his freedom, on the ground that he had lived for some years in free states and that Fort Snelling was on soil which Congress, by the Missouri Compromise, had declared forever free.

If the Supreme Court did not want to handle a hot potato it had an easy way out. It could hold that Scott as a slave could not be a citizen and so could not sue in federal court, and it could also hold that it was his status in Missouri that determined whether he was a slave or a free man. But the interesting part about the case was the Missouri

THE DAWNING OF THE LEAK

Often the main conduit for an inspired leak has been the press, and sometimes this has given rise to swelling freshets of public agitation. None, however, caused more of a flash flood than the earliest major leak in the nation's history. In the summer of 1795 the Philadelphia newspaper *Aurora* printed a copy of a treaty negotiated by Chief Justice John Jay with the government of Great Britain. Its disclosure outraged the Senate, which had voted to keep the treaty secret until mutually ratified by both nations; it also threw the country into a furor because most citizens felt that Jay had been altogether too subservient to the British with regard to American commerce, freedom of the seas, British posts in the West, and other sensitive matters. George Washington said that public reaction to the treaty, after the leak, was "like that against a mad dog"; frenzied mobs gathered in both the North and the South to shout down the document; Alexander Hamilton was pelted with stones when he tried to defend it in New York; Jay himself, someone observed, could have walked from one end of the country to the other at midnight by the light of fires burning him in effigy.

It turned out that Virginia's Senator Stevens T. Mason, a sturdy anti-Federalist, had handed a copy of the treaty to Pierre Adét, French minister to the United States. Since his country was at war with England and hated the idea of a treaty of "amity" between her and the United States, Adét gave the document to Benjamin Bache, publisher of the *Aurora*, with the hope of raising just the sort of public outcry that ensued—and even, perhaps, of blocking ratification of the treaty.

Although Federalist apologists rallied to the defense of Jay's treaty, and the country calmed down considerably, there was a tough struggle in the House of Representatives over whether to support the treaty— narrowly won, in the end, by the Federalists. The deliberate leak had served the purpose of venting publicly a controversial issue, and causing widespread discussion (as well as many a fist fight) in a manner that can only be described as aggressively democratic.

Compromise angle. Did Congress have the power to legislate freedom in a territory? If it did not, the old Missouri Compromise was dead; furthermore, if Congress could not prohibit slavery in a territory, the territory itself—a creature of Congress—could not do so either; in which case Senator Douglas' Popular Sovereignty plan was as dead as Moses . . . and in which case, also, Mr. Buchanan would be off of a cruel hook.

So in the weeks before his inauguration the President-elect undertook to open a leak. He wrote to his friend Justice James Catron asking how the court was going to rule, and when Justice Catron, after stalling briefly, indicated that the odds were favorable and suggested that Buchanan write also to Justice Robert Grier, Buchanan did so. Grier replied that he had shown the letter to Chief Justice Roger B. Taney and Justice James M. Wayne, and that "we fully appreciate and concur in your views as to the desirableness at the time of having an expression of the opinion of the Court on this troublesome question." This was plain as a pikestaff; the court was going to make a sweeping ruling on the whole broad question of slavery in the territories, and knowing the justices as he did, Buchanan had no doubt at all what the ruling was going to say.

Fortified by advance knowledge, then, Buchanan in his inaugural referred to the vexing question of slavery in the territories. This, he said, was "a judicial question, which legitimately belongs to the Supreme Court of the United States, before whom it is now pending and will, it is understood, be speedily and finally settled." With unctuous rectitude he went on to say: "To their decision, in common with all good citizens, I shall cheerfully submit."

Sure enough, two days later the court handed down its decision, declaring that nobody anywhere could keep slavery out of a territory; whereby it knocked out the Missouri Compromise, destroyed Douglas' Popular Sovereignty idea, and brought the nation a long step nearer to its most terrible war.

It was all a little too obvious: Buchanan had so clearly known what the answer was going to be when he piously called on his countrymen to abide by the court's findings. The Republicans loudly charged that the President and the Chief Justice had been conspiring together; and while this was not true, the President had exposed himself as a weakling who had schemed ineptly. He had succeeded only in splitting the Democratic Party.

A half century later a stronger President was at least partly involved in a leak of a very different sort, with a happier result.

In the early 1900's the American people were proud of their navy, which was quite new. It was being built up as fast as President Theodore Roosevelt could persuade Congress to act, it had recently destroyed two Spanish squadrons in spectacular one-sided battles, and it enjoyed a worldwide reputation for its fine marksmanship. But in 1902 President Roosevelt had on his desk a letter from an unhappy young officer enclosing two detailed reports indicating that the fine new ships were in fact dangerously inferior because of poor design, that the prized marksmanship was actually atrocious, and that the Navy Department was so badly organized that it could neither admit nor correct these flaws. He added that the promotion system was just about guaranteed to bring mediocrity to the top commands.

This was disturbing stuff, and there was not much the President could do about it just then; most of the reforms called for would take extensive acts of Congress, which was inclined to be quite happy with a navy that was so good-looking and had recently been so victorious, and never at any time does Congress enjoy having a President tell it how to legislate about the Navy. One thing Roosevelt could do on his own hook, and this he immediately did; he took the officer who had complained so sharply, Lieutenant William S. Sims, and appointed him inspector of target practice.

Sims performed excellently. He had no place to go but up. At the famous Battle of Santiago the American fleet had fired 9,500 projectiles, of which exactly 123 hit Spanish ships—and in the course of a few years Sims had changed things so that the Navy really did rank with the best in the business as far as gunnery was concerned. But on the other points no reform had been made or even attempted, and Sims was getting restless. So, in 1904, he sat down with a friend, a marine artist named Henry Reuterdahl, and gave him the material in the two interdepartmental reports that he had forwarded to the President. This, he cautioned, was not to be published just yet; Reuterdahl was to keep it on the back burner and wait until Sims gave him the go-ahead.

This came, at last, in 1907, when the end of Roosevelt's time in the White House was approaching and the Navy was much in the public eye on account of the battle fleet's famous cruise around the world. Sims told Reuterdahl to print his story whenever he could arrange it, and in January, 1908, it came out in *McClure's Magazine*, one of the most aggressive mass-circulation publications of that period.

It made a huge splash. American battleships, it asserted, were so badly designed that their armor belts were actually below the water line. They suffered from low freeboard to such an extent that in any kind of rough weather they could not fight their guns. Open shafts led from turrets to magazines, so that a fire or explosion in a turret could blow up the whole ship. (How serious this sort of defect could be was shown eight years later at Jutland, when a similar flaw led to the destruction of three British battle cruisers.) And the Navy's famous system of Bureaus was incredibly inefficient—so much so that no seagoing officer ever had anything to say about the design or construction of warships, which were in the hands of shoreside technicians answerable only to the Secretary of the Navy, whose knowledge of how ships ought to be put together depended entirely on what these technicians told him.

All in all, this was quite a bill of goods, and top brass was indignant. The Navy had a regulation forbidding officers to publish, directly or indirectly, information about acts or measures of the department, and Reuterdahl obviously had had access to those reports Sims had written several years earlier. The Secretary of the Navy sent Sims a severe letter remarking on the "very unusual similarity" between the magazine article and the supposedly secret reports, and Sims took the letter to the White House and showed it to President Roosevelt.

It is possible to suspect that Roosevelt had either put Sims up to giving Reuterdahl the reports in the first place or had at least carefully looked the other way while it was being done. In any case, he now gave Sims a light pat on the wrist and then held a sheltering wing over him while the admirals blew up a storm. Sims went on to win promotion, and when the United States entered the First World War he became commander of U.S. naval forces in European waters. Meanwhile a Senate committee investigated the Reuterdahl article in the full glare of publicity (which was exactly what Sims had hoped for), and the complaints about the Navy's defects were out where naval officers and taxpayers alike were bound to see them and take thought about them.

It would be nice to report that this set everything right, but things don't often work out so neatly. Reform came slowly—the cumbersome Bureau system was not greatly changed for many years—and the next few battleships that were designed still had all of the shortcomings Sims had been complaining about. But in time the reforms did come, better design was attained, and seven or eight years later American battleships were recognized on both sides of the Atlantic as leading the pack in plan and performance. When the real showdown finally came, the Navy was precisely the instrument America needed.

One of the most noteworthy dustups about the publication of forbidden information came in 1932, when a man named Herbert Yardley wrote a book on the way the United States had learned how to uncover Japanese military secrets. Yardley knew what he was talking about—he had been head of the intelligence division known as the Black Chamber during and after the First World War, and after Secretary of State Henry L. Stimson closed this project in 1929 with the remark that "gentlemen do not read each other's mail," Yardley had written an extremely indiscreet book about what had been done, naming nineteen nations whose secret codes the Black Chamber people had solved.

This was unfortunate, because a number of these nations promptly changed their codes, and when Yardley did his book on the Japanese, various people in the government felt that he ought to be stopped. At one time United States marshals seized the manuscript of his book on the ground that it violated a statute relating to the sanctity of secret documents, but nothing came of this and early in the New Deal administration a new law was devised providing fines and imprisonment for any government employee who published or connived at the publication of material prepared in a diplomatic code to which he, as a government worker, had had access.

The Senate was mildly puzzled, apparently inclined to wonder why the government needed to "create a new crime." Senator Tom Connolly of Texas, guiding the bill for the administration, had a quick reply: "All the bill would do is simply to make it a criminal offense for a scoundrel to betray his confidential relationship with the Government." In addition, it provided that anyone else who conspired with a government agent to use confidential material "for private gain or private profit ought to be punished." That seemed reasonable—after all, nobody can object to punishing scoundrels—and in the end the bill was passed, going on the statute books as Section 952 of Title 18, United States Code. But Senator Hiram Johnson looked toward the future and expressed a certain worry. This bill, he said, would not touch the particular offense it was aimed at (Yardley's) but would remain on the statute books . . . "a criminal law with harsh penalties, until—far in the future, when its original purpose will have been forgotten—it will be used for another purpose for which it was never intended and may do gross wrong."

Both senators, of course, were right, as far as men can be right in a politically uncertain world, and the two points of view on leakage of government information are still valid. There are government files, dossiers, memoranda, and so on that ought to remain hidden; some secrets are like phosphorus in that they burst into flame when exposed to the air. So governments are forever trying to devise laws that will protect the sanctity of such matters.

. . . and yet; pass such a law today and it will fly up and hit you in the face a generation later, when some situation you could not possibly have foreseen (l'affaire Watergate may be a case in point) generates the explosive force that will drive it out into the open. Sometimes the national welfare demands the publication of knowledge that was supposedly suppressed for the nation's good.

And this perhaps is another way of saying that over the long haul too much knowledge is better than too little. Democracy's road is always bumpy but it is the only road we have, and if it bruises us at times we at least keep moving. The leaks that cause these bumps now and then seem unendurable, but now and then they are also utterly essential. ☆

"A VOICE ONE HEARS ONCE IN A HUNDRED YEARS"

An Interview with

Marian Anderson

by Barbara Klaw

Conductor Arturo Toscanini said of her that she had "a voice one hears once in a hundred years." When she sang for composer Jean Sibelius at his home in Finland, he threw his arms around her, said, "My roof is too low for you," and called for champagne. Later he dedicated a song to her. She sang at President Kennedy's inauguration; President Johnson in 1963 presented her with the Presidential Medal of Freedom, America's highest civilian honor; and at the nation's two-hundredth anniversary celebration in Philadelphia on July 4, 1976, she was chosen to read the Declaration of Independence in the presence of President Ford.

But for Marian Anderson, this recognition of her extraordinary talent did not come easily. Much of America in the 1920's and 30's did not readily open its arms to a Negro singer.

She was born in Philadelphia at the turn of the century and began singing as a child in church choirs. At twenty she made her debut at Town Hall in New York but was so discouraged by unfavorable reviews that she almost dropped the whole idea of a singing career. In 1925 she was chosen from among three hundred contestants to sing with the New York Philharmonic Orchestra at Lewisohn Stadium in New York City. In spite of reviews that characterized her voice as "remarkable," the success that might have been expected did not follow, and like many other black performers she went to Europe to study and sing.

Scandinavians were the first to recognize this young contralto, whose voice has been compared to velvet, and she later sang to glowing acclaim in all the countries of Europe except Germany. (Early in the Hitler regime, she was asked to sing there, until a singularly uninformed manager wrote asking for assurance that she was 100 per cent Aryan. That concert was quickly cancelled.)

It was only when she was taken on by the flamboyant impresario Sol Hurok, however, that she managed to win over her own countrymen. Even Hurok's promotional skills could not easily overcome America's race prejudice. In 1939 the Daughters of the American Revolution refused to let her sing in their Constitution Hall in Washington, and Eleanor Roosevelt was so angered that she resigned from the organization. Instead, the federal government offered the Lincoln Memorial as the site for an outdoor performance on Easter Sunday, and she sang an unforgettable concert—including Schubert's Ave Maria and a selection of Negro spirituals—before seventy-five thousand people. This whole event, emotional for both audience and singer, established Miss Anderson firmly in the symbolic role in which she was always to be uncomfortable.

In 1955 Rudolf Bing, the director of New York's Metropolitan Opera, invited her to sing the part of Ulrica in Verdi's A Masked Ball. She was the first member of her race to be a soloist at the Opera, an honor accorded her—and the opera company—when she was well past the age at which singers normally make operatic debuts. She toured Asia for the State Department in 1957 and served as a U.S. delegate to the United Nations in 1958.

In 1965 she officially retired, and except for an occasional benefit or memorial for a friend, she has not sung publicly since.

In private life Marian Anderson is Mrs. Orpheus Fisher, and she and her husband live on a farm—the Mariana Farm—in Danbury, Connecticut, where they raise beef cattle. Her husband, nicknamed "King," is a retired architect.

Marian Anderson would never have picked for herself the role of activist in the fight for Negro equality. A calm, reserved, and essentially private person, she is generous in her judgment of the motives of others and singularly lacking in bitterness. But in pursuing her career she was constantly forced to challenge racial barriers simply to succeed as a singer. And this she has done—quietly, with dignity, and without fanfare. Recently she talked at length with a reporter from AMERICAN HERITAGE about the events and struggles of her life.

*   *   *   *   *   *

What was your childhood like?

A loveable one. I had a most attentive mother. In the family there was always love and joy and that was something I took for granted, because I was young.

Your father died when you were small, didn't he?

I was about nine, and it was traumatic because we thought he was quite something. He was tall and very fine looking and oh, how happy he was on holidays to take us out. He'd plan a picnic and I remember him so clearly getting things together for our outings.

Was it a difficult childhood economically?

Not really. I do believe we had things that we actually needed. My father did two or three things. He once had a coal and ice business. I say business, but he didn't have a store. He sold coal and he sold ice. Mother was a young woman when he died, and she could have done things quite differently. I mean she could have put us in a home, as was suggested to her, but she decided to keep us together.

Were you always interested in music?

Yes. When I was six years old I was taken to the church and I sang in the children's choir. And also about then somebody took me to a concert, and this was a Negro orchestra and the violinist came forward and played a solo, and I thought, that's for me. The big thing then for making money was scrubbing steps, so I scrubbed steps and I would get five cents or ten cents, or whatever. I did steps for four or five different people. Finally I saw a violin in a pawn shop and my aunt [Mary Prichard] went with me and I think it cost all of three dollars or a little more. But in any case, I happened to have saved that much money at the time, and I—how naive can you get?—I asked the man in the pawnshop if it was a good violin. Of course he said yes.

Well, I'll tell you, I didn't have a teacher for it, I never had even one lesson, but I learned to play so many things on it—sometimes all on one string. I'd go up as high as I could go and as low as it could go, and strings would break and I almost lost the bridge.

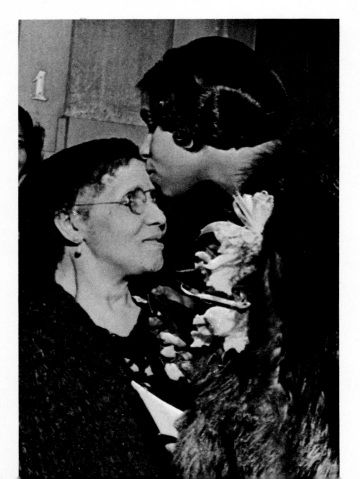

From the time I was a very small child, music always got my attention. I remember our room in school was next to the room where the children were learning songs. I didn't always do my lesson as well as I might have done had that music class not been next door, but I learned all the songs being taught in there.

How did you become a singer?

First there was the children's choir at church. My mother was a Methodist and my father was a Baptist, so we were between two churches. At eleven, I sang in the senior choir and got wonderful experience. It wasn't long after I was in the choir that the director would let me take home all the music that was going to be used the next Sunday, and I learned everybody's part. The bass, of course, I sang an octave higher. I had no inhibitions about doing high C's or anything at all.

And then as I grew, my aunt and I tripped to two or three different churches in the same evening. I wasn't engaged for it, but my aunt might see somebody in the street and they'd say, look, we're having a this, that, or the other on Wednesday night. Could you bring Marian? And my auntie would go there and I would go with her and there'd be a song or two. And sometimes one of the ladies might come and give me one dollar or whatever. If we went to two or three churches, I might make three or four dollars, sometimes less than that, scarcely more.

What did you do with those vast sums?

It wasn't a difficult thing. By this time my father was dead, and so the money was given to my mother for my sisters and me.

When did you turn from being a singer in church choirs in Philadelphia to being simply a singer?

It happened very gradually. Some churches were too small to have a concert there, so someone in the church would engage a small hall for a money-raising affair. Once in a while we would get a reporter to come to a concert, and he would write a notice. Gradually the churches were larger, the halls were larger. The minister at our church—the Union Baptist Church—invited Roland Hayes [a famous Negro tenor], the one big attraction that drew people from all over the city. At that point, Roland Hayes was opening his programs with Italian classics and German lieder, and maybe a French art song. My claim to fame was that I was singing English only, and the people would say, "If our Marian sings, at least we will know what she's singing about."

Were you studying singing by then?

Yes, I had a voice teacher, my first teacher, who was Mary Saunders Patterson. She was a person in the neighborhood and she had a gorgeous voice. She had a large class of young people whom she was teaching, and she took me in without getting paid. I was in high school then, and later somebody offered to pay for my lessons and Mrs. Patterson did accept this, but she charged only a dollar a lesson. Can you imagine?

Miss Anderson leans down to kiss her mother after a concert at Philadelphia's Academy of Music in 1937.

What was the first triumph of your career?

It was probably a contest in Lewisohn Stadium in New York in which three hundred people took part. I was out of high school by then. Out of the three hundred contestants, they chose sixteen. From the sixteen, four were to be chosen, and from the four, one.

What was the number you sang?

"O Mio Fernando" from Donizetti's *La Favorita*. Before my turn came, that song had been sung already six times. The teacher I was studying with then had said no matter what the judges do—they have those little steel things that they make a noise with if they have heard enough—don't you stop until you get to the end. At the end I had a trill which he thought wasn't bad. Fortunately, they didn't try to stop me.

Did you have disappointments as well as triumphs?

Oh, yes. I had a very big disappointment. The teacher decided it was time I had a recital on my own.

Where was the recital to be?

At Town Hall in New York, my first Town Hall appearance, as they say, the real big one. My teacher put together a program in which there were four German lieder. I sang this German phonetically, and the notices were not very good. The critics said Marian Anderson sang her German as if by rote. And I was extremely disappointed. I took it very much to heart, I suppose because I knew they were absolutely right, you know. It was a great shock. Anyway, I didn't sing in public for more than a year after that.

Did you consider giving up your singing career?

I was really that much discouraged. I was trying to get rid of everything that pertained to music as much as possible. I just said, all right, that part of my life is finished.

My mother said to me, you must remember that nobody has one hundred per cent acceptance of what they do. No one is perfect. If there were people who were perfect they would have been taken up above long ago.

Then came the time when I couldn't stand it any longer and I just absolutely had to go back to singing.

In your singing career, have you encountered much discrimination?

Yes, I've encountered discrimination. You can't do without it. I mean, you could very well do without it.

I understand there was an incident in a music school in Philadelphia.

It was a tremendously great shock, and I was very unprepared. I went into this music school to see about applying. There at the window was this beautiful girl, and I thought, she has everything, she has beauty, she's here in a school where she hears music every day, it's just wonderful. I was standing in line and when I got almost to the window she looked past me to the person in back of me. Then she did this again. Finally she said, "What do you want?" I said, "I would like to have a brochure, please." And she said, "We don't take colored." And she said it as if . . . she *liked* saying it, you know. So you learn. I don't say you ever accept, but you learn that there are people who are like that. . . .

As the sorceress, Ulrica, in Verdi's *A Masked Ball*, Miss Anderson rehearses with the Metropolitan Opera in 1955.
U.P.I.

Is the memory of that still hurtful to you?

I don't really think it is because . . . for two reasons: the first reason being it wouldn't be done today. And the other is that if it should happen, children are so knowledgeable now that they would not be as bowled over by it as I was then.

When you began to travel as a singer, did you encounter much discrimination? What about trains, for instance?

Well, there were certain places on trains where my people were supposed to stay that were not conducive to sleeping or anything else. If the porter was friendly enough or knew the Pullman porter, they might at night, when people were already in bed, give you a lower berth if they had an extra on the train. So I could get to sleep. But I was always anxious to get out of it in the morning before other people were up.

Sometimes they would give you berth 13. Berth 13 was a drawing room. That was special treatment. The thing is you had your own bathroom in berth 13. In the regular berths, the bathroom at the end of the car took care of two or three people at the same time, and you would probably be in there when someone else came in, and I don't know what unpleasant incidents could or would take place. . . .

Somebody doesn't always come right up to you and say, "You can't have this, you can't have that." It's just as though there's a hair that blows across your face. Nobody sees it, but it's there and you can feel it.

53

What about traveling in the South?

What you did then was to change trains in Washington. Somebody would come through the train and make an announcement: "Coming into Washington, coming into Washington." In Washington you got on another train to go south and there was a special coach on there for my people. It's all so unbelievable that other human beings can be so small. One doesn't change as a person from Philadelphia to Washington!

Could you get hotel accommodations in the South then?

No, one could not. I always had to have the manager seek somebody in the Negro section who had enough room so that I might be a guest while I was there for the concert. These families were as lovely to me as they could possibly be, but I didn't, of course, have the peace and quiet that I would have had in a hotel.

What about the audiences at Southern concerts? Were they segregated?

Yes, I sang before segregated audiences for a while. And then I didn't do it anymore. I said I wouldn't come back until things were different. In one city, they put the box seats in a hall at the disposal of my people. Of course, these are much more expensive than the other seats.

Did you have to stop singing in the South?

We lost a few concerts. When seats were made available anywhere in the hall for anyone who had the money to pay for them, then we went back.

Do you feel the South has changed a lot?

Oh, I'm certain of that, my dear. I want to tell you about something that happened. There was one hotel that never would take me, and it caused great difficulty in that particular place. Well, the last time we went South I was booked into that hotel. I was given a room with a bay window, and a huge bedroom, and then a sort of dressing room, and it was very, very nice. When I went down to pay my bill in the morning, the lady behind the desk said, "Look here" . . . and my heart began to pound, and I thought, now what is this? She said, "When you come down here again, don't you go no place but here."

It was the nicest thing you can imagine. Now that person might have been there all the time, but never had the opportunity to say that.

You have a reputation for being very calm as a performer. Are you naturally a calm person?

Well, I believe that I am a calm person. You know, some performers say, Oh, I'm scared to death, but I don't believe I'm like that. My feeling is this, that if one is prepared to do the best she can under all circumstances, all the worry that might go on inside your head, or inside your body, won't help a bit. It will hinder you.

Would you say then that you don't suffer from stage fright?

I wouldn't say that. I think you have to have a certain excitement, a certain anxiety, before you get out on the stage, because if you don't it can be just an everyday affair.

It could be that singing in the church, which was a very large church in Philadelphia, allowed me to get used to standing and performing before people when I was very young. Some people study for eight or ten years, and then at their debut concert it's the first time they've appeared before the type of audience which wants to find out for itself what Mary Jones is all about. Performers are tremendously concerned about that first audience. But my first audience, in church, was a huge one.

Why did you always sing with your eyes closed?

At first it was to close out everything. To turn myself in, you know, and to close out distractions. Sometimes you get an audience and some people are talking in the second, third row and that troubles you because you want to get to that person and you haven't made it yet. Just automatically the eyes close and you have pictures in your head.

How do you approach an audience?

Well, my mother always said to me, "Remember when you go out on the stage, you've already made an impression before you've even opened your mouth to sing a note." And that advice has stood me in good stead.

Do you sing to some particular person or group?

Yes, absolutely, and you know it's amazing how you can stand there and you can literally read on the faces of people in the front rows whether they came to the concert of their own free will or if somebody sort of pushed them into going, or if they got a free ticket. And it's a very satisfying thing to look out at one of those people when you have finished a song and find that the person has become interested. I am there to satisfy them and give them something I'd like to share.

You were first successful in Europe. Weren't you tempted to stay? What made you come back?

It's home. My mother was a wonderful, unassuming person. She was not a fighter, she didn't talk loud. I never heard her voice raised in anger, but all through the years,

Mother was always there. One of the things that made me happiest in my life was that I could eventually tell Mother, who worked hard every day, that she didn't have to work anymore. She was a cleaning lady at Wanamaker's, and she had been ill, and the doctor suggested that she stay home one particular morning. So I called up the head of the department and I said, "This is Marian Anderson, and my mother will not be coming in any more to work." My mother was a person on whom they put the hardest things to do. I used to come from high school down to Wanamaker's, and Mother would be digging in some little corner, feeling that the existence of the store depended on how clean she got that corner.

I would have come back from anywhere to my family.

What did singing spirituals mean to you?

Well, I had never lived in the South, and when I was young spirituals seemed to me to have come from the Deep South and away back. I knew I loved them, they meant something to me, but how they were rendered, where they came from, was a different thing. I know my aunt asked me one time, why did I have to sing spirituals. She didn't care for spirituals at all. She didn't consider the spirituals beautiful music, and they brought back to her the hideous things that had happened to the Negro. You know, so many of the songs deal with Heaven and the Lord and the day when you get up yonder—I'll be there, I'll be waiting for you, and Oh Lord, how come me here, wish I'd never been born.

But I felt differently. I'd heard Roland Hayes sing them with the seriousness he did, and I knew that he had something within him that understood their meaning. I'd see

At John Kennedy's inauguration in 1961, Marian Anderson sings the National Anthem flanked by an array of Presidents and First Ladies—past, present, and future. At her right are Mmes. Eisenhower, Johnson, and Kennedy, ex-President Eisenhower, and President-elect Kennedy. At her left are future Presidents Johnson and Nixon, and the Trumans.

people in the church, they'd clap their hands, tap the knee, and have their rhythm and sing their songs, and they didn't need anything else. The music can be written down, but if you live where spirituals are sung and people give vent to their feelings then you'll hear a note here and a note there which is not on paper. Have you ever heard the records of Mahalia Jackson? Well, listening to her records, there are all kinds of little things that cannot be put down on paper but come out of the soul, the heart and soul of the singer.

I must tell you about going to a meeting, a meeting in a huge tent.

A revival meeting?

Yes, unbelievable! Maybe two or three thousand people, or maybe even more. I was young when I first went to one, just a short way out of Philadelphia. There were some people just talking, talking and then they would start a hymn. You couldn't hear all over the place, impossible, because it was too large, but like in a field of swaying corn, or wheat, a ripple would come your way, and you could hear voices, you could hear that it was music. Then it got nearer and nearer until you were engulfed in it. Somebody else takes it up and sings another verse and the song goes on and on and still like a wheat field the audience begins to move this way and that, to sway.

Four-voice, four-part harmony—it was absolutely, unbelievably gorgeous, gorgeous in your ear.

Y*ou always included some spirituals in your programs, didn't you? Which one did you sing most often?*

"He's Got the Whole World in His Hands," and another I love particularly, about Negroes being despondent—"Oh Lord, How Come Me Here."

Sol Hurok became your manager in 1935. Did he remain your manager from then on?

Yes, and I still have a contract which he sent me to sign years ago. I never signed it. We didn't have a contract for years, but I had a manager for years. He used to enjoy telling people that I wouldn't even sign his contract.

He sounds like a fascinating man. Was he a good manager?

He was for *me*. It depends on how you knew the man. The experience of meeting him was to me a great thing because I had tried so desperately to meet him in New York. Impossible! Several people tried to arrange it but it was impossible. But I was singing in Paris one night, the Salle Gaveau, I believe it was, and he came backstage in the intermission and said, "I want to see you tomorrow morning." So we went, and he was sitting behind a very large desk and his arms were out, like that, and he looked like a colossus.

Was he a very large man?

Not as large as I saw him, large and much larger than life. It was a terrific thing for my accompanist and me and before we left him that morning he said that he would like to manage some concerts for us when we came back to America. We were already under management in New York, and he wanted to know exactly how many concerts we had scheduled. It turned out there were only two concerts planned, and one of those was at my sorority. Mr. Hurok said that he would offer seven concerts and that

we could have a few others if they went well. So I had a series of fifteen concerts that season.

And that was the first year?

Yes, and from then on he added and added and added until one season we had ninety concerts. That was really too much. We couldn't keep that up all the time, but I generally did from ten to twelve or thirteen concerts a month.

Mr. Hurok did some things, a particular thing, that I thought was a little much. Some organizations get their whole series of artists from a particular manager, and they are sometimes at a loss to know whom to put in a place that might be left vacant [because of illness]. Mr. Hurok simply said, in this case, I would like you to engage [Marian Anderson]. The message came back that their roster was suddenly full. I heard that he said, well, all right, then maybe next year you don't want to have so-and-so—the person who had been their main attraction for years.

A little pressure, right?

Well, one of my race had never performed there and while I feel at that point Mr. Hurok wasn't looking at me so much as a Negro as he was looking at me as an attraction, I think that was the basis on which he was working.

Hurok must have had to deal frequently with the problem of race, particularly at the beginning, didn't he?

That's right, and I'm quite sure it came up more often than I would ever know.

You don't think he told you about such incidents?

No, because as in the Washington affair . . .

The D.A.R. concert at Constitution Hall?

Yes. I was not aware of what was going on until one morning, in San Francisco, as I stood waiting for the cable car, I happened to turn around to a newsstand and I saw "Mrs. Roosevelt resigns from the D.A.R. because . . ." and then I saw "Marian Anderson" there. I didn't know about it then.

Some of the press was very disappointed when I couldn't tell them step by step what had happened. They kept asking questions until we got to Washington.

Do you think Mr. Hurok had been purposely trying to shield you, or do you think it was just because you were all the way across the country?

I was a long way away but also he was a very astute man and he knew I couldn't do anything to help.

Wasn't it very upsetting, though?

Well, when I first knew about it, it was. Music to me means so much, such beautiful things, and it seemed impossible that you could find people who would curb you, stop you, from doing a thing which is beautiful. I wasn't trying to sway anybody into any movements or anything of that sort, you know.

How did you feel about the performance at the Lincoln Memorial?

It was a tremendous thing and my heart beat like mad—it's never beat like that before—loud and strong and as though it wanted to say something, if you know what I mean. I don't like to use the word protesting but my reaction was, what have I done that should bring this onto my heart? I was not trying to cut anybody down. I just wanted to sing and to share.

You never sang in opera until 1935, did you? Were you anxious to sing opera?

Oh, yes, indeed. To come home from high school, we had to go under a railroad trestle and the trains would be rolling along. And I remember thinking, "Oh, if just one of these days I could be on a train with the Metropolitan Opera Company going somewhere." And I prayed to the evening star, and I prayed and I prayed. So I had dreamed about it for a very long time—from high school days through the better part of my career. Finally when the opportunity came, how nonchalantly it was proposed! I saw Mr. Bing [at a party at Sol Hurok's]. He came up to me and said, "How would you like to sing at the Met?" as nonchalantly as you can imagine. My heart was beating so fast and so loudly that I could scarcely hear what else was said. I did make out, however, "Did you ever sing——?" After that I didn't know what name he was saying. I said, "Well, no, I really haven't." That answer would have been true for any opera because I hadn't sung opera.

Hₒw did it go?

It was a tremendous experience for me. I've never found the right words to explain what I felt about all that. I wasn't ready for all those trimmings, so many people moving about at the same time, you know, and being one little segment of something. It was so joyful. I only wished that it had come earlier in life when I might have been able to bring more to it.

Were you readily accepted by the other members of the company?

Yes, I made some wonderful friends there. To describe what the feeling was, the first day I appeared at the stage door, there were cameras all over the place. It was a moment of speechlessness for me. And the first thing I heard when I got inside was a man, a stagehand, who said to me, "Welcome home."

Your singing career was a very long one. Do singers' voices normally stay at their peak that long, or were you particularly lucky?

I might have been lucky, and yet I do believe that as the body begins to slow, slant, deteriorate—whatever one wants to say—the mechanism that singers must use can be affected by this decline. When I was young, I could put my head back a little, and sing high C without any trouble at all. I wouldn't attempt a high C today unless I worked a very great deal. I have no idea how long a person should be able to sing, but I know there are some who sang very very many years longer than I did.

Does the thought of age bother you?

Not really. Of course, I don't run upstairs two at a time like I used to. But if you realize you've had an active life, you don't have to prove it now to anybody.

I have noticed that nothing written about you ever gives your age.

No.

Before the statue of Lincoln at the Lincoln Memorial, Marian Anderson sings her famous 1939 Easter concert.

And yet, there is going to be a special concert this month—sponsored by Young Audiences, *in honor of your seventy-fifth birthday, isn't that right?*

Yes. I just decided, not really decided, but I was thinking whether or not I would let them have the concert at seventy-five or what, but that's what they said they were planning. It reminds me of Mr. Hurok. Somebody said, Now, Mr. Hurok, we'd like to do this for you but we have to know how old you are. So he said, Yes. Just yes. And then after a while they said, You know, everyone says that you're such and such a number of years old. And he said, All right, let them say it.

So you're not guaranteeing anything?

[Laughing] No. No indeed.

In your autobiography you say, "I would be fooling myself to think I was meant to be a fearless fighter." What did you mean by that?

Certainly I have my feelings about conditions that affect my people. But it is not right for me to try to mimic somebody who writes, or who speaks. That is their forte. I think first of music and of being there where music is, and of music being where I am. What I had was singing, and if my career has been of some consequence, then that's my contribution. ☆

57

The Terror of the Wilderness

A despairing human being, swept helplessly toward destruction, is Thomas Cole's vision of **Manhood** *in his series,* **The Voyage of Life,** *1840. In Cole's allegory, nature is seen as the early settlers saw it—as malignant—and man's hope is in a remote spirit, upper left.*

by Frederick Turner

rceived nature as something to be conquered?

Most people who have reflected at all upon the known history of the Americas, particularly North America, have been impressed one way or another with its dominant quality of fierceness. After that early, first blush of paradisial imaginings, stained by the lush colors of the tropic islands and the defenseless peoples found thereon, a somber mood of misgiving settled over the questing Europeans, filtered their perceptions, filtered at last into the bleached bones of their accounts of exploration. This was not paradise after all, but a tangled, hostile wilderness which had to be savaged to the extent that it was itself savage.

By the time of the establishment of the English colonies it was simply standard to describe America as a "fierce and howling wilderness" peopled by the skulking, interchangeable forms of wolves and savages, and it is not the mere tribute of chronological antiquity that has made William Bradford's *History of Plymouth Plantation* a classic of our literature: Bradford's narrative bristles like a wilderness itself with the adjectival reactions of a civilization's enraged, baffled disappointment with the lands it had found. What *could* they see, as Bradford so rightly asks, "but a hideous and desolate wilderness, full of wild beasts and wild men?" No solace to be had from such lands, such peoples, a whole country "full of woods and thickets, represent[ing] a wild and savage hue."

Later observers, coming after Bradford, after the settlements had been perilously established, then defended, and finally extended ever deeper into the wild gloom, remarked not only on that gloom but on the fierceness of the settlements and the settlers themselves. Astonished Britishers and Frenchmen described the wild haste and abandon with which these New World pioneers pursued their work as well as their sports, bolting gigantic quantities of steaming food, draining flagons of fiery punch or rum. Before the spectacle of New World civilization the representatives of the Old flinched in awe.

And then, of course, there was that fierce hand-to-hand combat always joined on the edges of the settlements, the combat with the vast, untamed wilderness itself. Foreign observers and American witnesses alike were astonished by the incredibly rapid transmogrification of a Stone Age landscape into that of a "civilized" nation—as Westerners had come to define that: settlements almost monthly hacked out of seemingly endless groves of timber; raw, palisaded stockades and cabins; towns hammered together on rolling grasslands like some ghostly precursors of instantly assembled movie sets; and, finally, in what Lewis Mumford has so rightly termed the ultimate assault on the natural world, the continent's rocky bed blasted and quarried; rivers dammed and bridged; railroad ties laid and clinched.

In addition, while all of this was changing the face of the continent, there was the ongoing, fiercely unremitting struggle with the aboriginal inhabitants, who resisted with equal ferocity the white incursions into their homeland.

All of which is now a commonplace assumption of our cultural heritage. We accept as natural our fierce history and its manifest consequences—our landscape, our popular heroes and sports, even our current position as gunrunners to the arsenals of the world.

A mythical South American sea monster, 1621

Like so much else in the history of the West this response to the New World and its aboriginal inhabitants is in part the bequest of Near Eastern antiquity. Living their hard, narrowly marginal existence in an environment that gave so little, and that but grudgingly, those ancient desert peoples naturally developed an abiding notion that Nature was in itself hostile to man's efforts to live. Particularly was this so of the seminomadic herdsmen whose deep ponderings and parched, leathered yearnings gave vent to the sacred traditions that were to be the spiritual lifeblood of Western civilization. Beyond their small settlements, their water, shade trees, and arable, improved land, lay darkness, dry desolation, death. Thus *Genesis*, which commences our spiritual history, dramatizes the adversary relationship of man and environment: man placed in a paradise strongly suggestive of a Mesopotamian walled garden and ordered to subdue his natural surroundings and establish dominion over them; man punished by expulsion from the lush garden into the inhospitable, threatening outer world where only sweat can mean bread. And thus also throughout the Old Testament—particularly in the Pentateuch where the mythology's basic creed is stated—wilderness is consistently used as a metaphor for spiritual decay, the darkness of nonexistence beyond the Lord's way, death itself: the Scapegoat, bearing its intolerable burden of collective guilt, is sent to the

wilderness, that wilderness itself out of which the Lord will deliver His people into the light and life of His protection. When Moses speaks to the nation, huddled on the plains of Moab and poised for an attack upon the pagan Canaanites, he reminds them that their God, His way, is life and civilization, all else wilderness, for it was the Lord who found Jacob in a desert land,

> and in the howling waste of the wilderness;
> he encircled him, he cared for him,
> he kept him as the apple of his eye.

Even that other biblical tradition of the wilderness as a place of spiritual refuge, retreat, to which eremitical holy men repaired to purify themselves and prepare the way—even this fed the stronger and older tradition of resistance to the wilderness, for in this case the wilderness was a testing ground and a place of temptation where the faithful must win out. It was not a locale that could be accepted on what might be its own terms, and certainly it held no secrets of the spirit for the Lord's people. Indeed, in Jewish folklore the wilderness as a place of temptation carries within it a strong sexual component, as in the passage from *Isaiah* where it is seen as the abode of Lillith, a wild-haired nymphomaniac prone to visiting unwary wanderers and tempting them into terrible, unholy alliances. Here again, the force of resistance must be at least as strong as the force of temptation if God's way was to win out. And so, if God did send His people out into these places of desolation, acceptance—or worse, surrender—meant death, the eternal rot of decay that was divine judgment against a fatal embrace. The mission then was more obviously to conquer and prevail out there and, in doing so, to harmonize these places with the rest of God's kingdom, i.e., civilization.

If from this ancient Near Eastern well we inherited a mythology that enjoined fear of and resistance to the wilderness, from our Greco-Roman inheritance we learned how to create both history and geography in our own image —not that these civilizations invented ethnocentric images of the world (as a glance at the Pentateuch would surely show), but they did indicate with considerable brilliance how ethnocentrism could become the ordering principle in descriptions of the world, its past, present, and future. History becomes what Western civilization makes happen. History is thus also that which happens to the primitive others that civilization encounters. They themselves can have no history—and no future, either.

Herodotus, that ceaseless old traveler, his ear to every wind of rumor as of fact, tells us that the Persians had themselves developed something of this principle, honoring their nearest neighbors (those most like Persians) the most, then those nearest these, and so on, "their respect decreasing as the distance grows. . . ." And so it was with the beginnings of our historiography and geography with the Greeks and Romans, in which development old Herodotus is himself deeply implicated. His respect for truth, not to say plausibility, decreased as he described lands and peoples farther and farther outside the Greek world.

Arthur O. Lovejoy and George Boas, in their monumental work on *Primitivism and Related Ideas in Antiquity*, concentrate on Greco-Roman notions of the admirable, even paradisial qualities of the primitives of the wilderness, and, of course, it is true that this is an ancient dream that man has not easily released: that somewhere else, back there in the precivilized past, harmony and spiritual peace lie buried and waiting. Yet in historical perspective it seems clear that these lingering, latent paradisial notions always yielded to the greater strength of the imperative to conquer the wilderness and to subdue its peoples.

And so, although Herodotus himself, the Father of History, betrays some primitivistic longings in his descriptions of the world, still more strongly do his histories demonstrate the ethnocentric bias, using Greek civilization as the reference point, the norm and apex, in relation to which the faraway lands and peoples become progressively monstrous. Thus we find that there are Indian tribes that rut in open fields like cattle, their sperm as black as their skins; a race of goat-footed men that inhabits a snarled mountain range beyond the farthest reaches of Scythia; a Libyian tribe that hunts a race of troglodytes in four-horse chariots. And still farther toward the dark, unknown West, scarcely a geographical direction really, there were horned asses, dog-headed men, headless men with eyes in their chests, wild women, a race with no individual names, only the tribal one, and men who squeaked like bats. "I don't vouch for this," Herodotus wrote, "but merely respect what the Libyans say."

Such, in brief, are the words our ancient mentors spoke to us. Such, skeletally, was the equipment with which Europeans had been provided for yet further thrusts outward into the West, into its girdle which the Arab geographers and mathematicians called "the Green Sea of Darkness" and of which they were themselves so mortally frightened. For it was the Arabs who were the conduit through which so much of that ancient bequest came to us, and learning through them we learned how to draw up maps that neatly divided the world into three sections, with "Europa" at the center. We learned, too, to draw up deeper, mental maps of existence in which, again, Europa was central, the barbarians at the borders, and the savages and their lands entirely off the edges. Beyond the walls of the city as locus of the light of civilization lay the azoic zones of darkness, anticivilization, nonhistory, death. Or, if not this last, then a mode of existence so free and unsponsored by God as to be terrible, irrational, insane.

Regarding this spiritual map, it seems useful to think of Freud and Jung, both of whom hypothesized that the radical experiences of a people's far past could be encoded within the minds of succeeding generations—though, of course, Freud could not accept Jung's theory of how such inheritances might be transmitted, preferring "memory traces" to Jung's "collective unconscious." Yet whatever these great minds' theoretical disagreement, it appears in this regard at least that the general thrust of their speculations is unassailable. Looking at Western civilization's historiography, cartography, iconography, and folk traditions during its Middle Ages, it seems clear that Westerners were critically, crucially unprepared for the looming encounter with the New World—unprepared by their very preparation. The experiences and the reactions of the old desert peoples, of the Greeks, of the Romans and their encounters with the savage tribes of Germany, the fenny landscape of Britain—all this had entered the mind and marrow of Western men, preparing them, captains and spear-carriers alike, to resist the New World and its inhabitants, insisting fiercely that every newness be made over into an older image or else be obliterated.

As just one example, though a crucial one to be sure, of what is meant here, let me mention the mental phenomenon of the Wild Man of the Middle Ages as he is described by Richard Bernheimer in his book of that title.

This hirsute figure of medieval folklore is a direct descendant of those ancient, shaggy satyrs and night demons who haunted the uncharted spaces of the mind of the Near East, and his image was strengthened in the folklore of Greco-Roman writers and their disciples, the early Christian cosmographers. The Wild Man, like the satyrs and demons, lived far from the light of civilization, lurking amidst the twisted shadows of the European outback. His life therein was so brutish as to be all but animalistic, and like the animals he was free of restraints and trammels, so free as to be insane. He had no knowledge of the True God—which is just a more precise definition of insanity—and he was darkly sexual in intention and inclination, desiring nothing so much as to carry off the fainting white maiden to his woody lair and marry her (in Bernheimer's euphemistic description). So large did this figure loom in the imagination of that time that his presence can be discerned in places as various as French romances, German minstrel songs, the words of Spenser and Cervantes, the tops of love caskets, on stove tiles, tapestries, candlestick holders, and drinking cups.

His significance here is simply this: that shocking and depraved though he is, bestial as may be his behavior, yet he bears some terrifying relationship to civilized man. Thus he must be either civilized or murdered.

Of course, it is clear now that the Wild Man was but the imaginary precursor of the very real American aborigines, and the spring festivals of a Europe as yet ignorant of those it would style "Indians" are dark with the promise of real capture and real genocide: for in them the symbolic pursuit and killing of the Wild Man prepares the way for the advent of spring itself. In a grotesque parody of primitive seasonal rituals, the civilized Westerner here paid unwitting tribute to his inherited belief that the death of wildness meant also the regeneration of life. The joyous dance of triumph over the remains of the Wild Man becomes the civilized analogue of the loathsome scalp dance.

Speculations such as these lead one almost inescapably to the conclusion that the truest way to regard the whole phenomenon of discovery and conquest here in the Americas is as a clash of mythologies. It is for this reason that the New World's first major historian, Flemish engraver-publisher Théodore de Bry, remains so significant a source of information about those first moments when whites stumbled across something they were not looking for. De Bry's engravings are crammed with the iconography of sixteenth-century Christian mythology. For example, in his justly celebrated engraving of Columbus on his first voyage out, the explorer's feet are planted resolutely on the planks of his ship, itself the culminating artifact of over a century of accelerated technological ingenuity, and he is shown armed with the other artifacts—the charts, armor, guns—that would make discovery and conquest possible, and armed also with the West's accumulated mythology, which would make conquest and destruction inevitable. In the setting history provided de Bry there is nothing really contradictory in the appearance here, on the flag the Admiral holds, of the Christian savior hanging from the cross of our regeneration, and the sea nymphs and sea monsters, the satyrs and griffins, who dance in the cross-hatched waves. Though there is nothing in the attitudes of these mythic figures to indicate a resistance to newness, yet in the posture of the Admiral himself there is a resoluteness, a settled sternness that could know nothing of surrender or even of humbled acceptance. Perhaps de Bry invests his central figure with the attitude he sensed in his civilization, or perhaps he simply had the benefit of a century of hindsight (the engraving appeared in 1594) and knew already how it had turned out with the New World, knew how perfectly appropriate it had been to have had this stiff-necked Genoese lead the first shocking assault upon those unsuspected, unsuspecting shores.

It is an expression of neither neoromanticism nor twentieth-century primitivism to remark that by contrast the mythologies of aboriginal America counsel acceptance of the natural world, wild or cultivated, and that though often in the presence of a newness that was terrifying, the aborigine was apt to find his salvation in surrender rather than in resistance. That, of course, is the essence of their myths of culture heroes, those men and women who set their faces and their steps away from the camps or towns, who went into the wildernesses of other worlds wherein they found themselves and so found the gods and their secrets of living. These myths, so central to the lives of the tribes, had their everyday analogues in the puberty rites and in the vision quests of individuals. In these, the questers faced their inner anxieties in isolation, drawing support and strength from their traditions which told them how spiritual triumph must come from within.

In this connection I have for some time been drawn to a myth of the Iroquois, that six-nation confederacy that has so much to tell us of the virtues, the high excellences, of the American aborigines, as it does also of the blackest depths of the human heart where cruel vengeance waits for release. In the tribal past, these fierce lords of the north woods probably practiced cannibalism, but they also had marvelous theories of dreams, grand statecraft and statesmen, and artistry in their beautiful embroidery. And this:

Once there was a young hunter lost in a snowstorm in the woods. Blinded by snowflakes and darkness falling through twisted tree trunks, he stumbled into the yet deeper blackness of a sheltering cave to wait there for light and the end of the storm. But suddenly out of its deepest recesses came the confused sounds of a demon: sounds of a singing stream suddenly changed to the mad tumble of a cataract; soft and then mournful sighs of wind. And then a huge, cavernous voice spoke to the awed hunter crouched at the cave's entrance. He had chanced into the abode of the last of the Stone Giants, cannibalistic predators who in the mythic past had all but destroyed the Iroquois with their carnivorous raids but who had themselves been destroyed through the intervention of Ta-ha-hia-wa-gon, Upholder of the Heavens. All but one. This one had crept away to this cave of desolation to live on in acts of monumental destructiveness, rearranging the Allegheny landscape in his fits of abandoned passion. None had seen him and lived to tell of it, for his very glance would turn one to stone. And yet the words he now spoke to the lone hunter, the words booming out of impossible depths, were not a death sentence but instead words imbued with life.

I shall spare you, the giant said, for I know you have come here in trouble and not to kill. And therefore I shall teach you great secrets. "From here you will go forth, free to live with the animals, the birds, and the fish. All these were your ancestors before you were human, and hereafter it will be your task to dedicate your life to their honoring!" The Stone Giant sent him on his way with these words:

> Be wise and learn my secrets,
> How disease is healed,
> How man and beast and plant may talk together
> And learn one another's missions.
> Go and live with the trees and birds and beasts and
>   fish,
> And learn to honor them as your own brothers.

It is perhaps impossible to make too much of such a narrative, for its fellows are found in the traditions of tribes all over the Americas, witnesses to the majesterial beauties, the tones, tempers, and moods of two vast and unscarred continents.

62

And yet these same features caused the newcomers to fear and resist this New World, its flora and fauna, and its inhabitants who succeeded—God knew how!—in living apparently unaided in the very heart of wildness.

Another fear must be added which is not primitive, only misguided—the betrayal of history. By this I mean that any real acceptance of the New World, any acceptance of the aborigines' independent existence, or, far worse, any desire to merge, mingle, *marry* the New World and its inhabitants—any of these attitudes or desires—were nothing less than surrenders to the temptations of the wilderness. Thus they had to be seen as betrayals of God's plan for human activity. They were betrayals of thousands of years of civilization, reversions from the path of history (that is, the record of the achievements of Western whites) into the jungle of pre- or anti-history.

And so no more loathsome object could be imagined in this New World phase of civilization's triumphant march than an individual who seemed to have surrendered to the call of the wild, to have met the New World on its turf, not on the geography of Europe.

In this light an apparently trivial incident recorded by Bernal Díaz del Castillo takes on the aspect of a key moment in the unfolding history of the Americas. This old soldier-turned-chronicler tells us that Cortés, moving toward the destruction of the Aztecs, stumbled across two Spaniards from an earlier, abortive, expedition. They were living with the Indians. One was brought to him, but before Cortés would recognize him he ordered him dressed in European clothing. So shocking was it how reduced this civilized man appeared. The other man, however, one Gonzalo Guerrero ("warrior" in Spanish), utterly refused to come before the leader, his own countryman. Instead he sent word out of the woods by way of the Indianized Spaniard Jerónimo de Aguilar that he was married and had three sons, that his body was tattooed and his lower lip pierced, and that the tribe considered him very brave. Worse, he was well pleased with his Indian life and had no desire to return to civilization. And, Jerónimo de Aguilar added, this Guerrero had actually advised his tribesmen to attack an earlier expedition at Cape Catoche. When Cortés learned all this he exclaimed that he wished he could get his hands on Guerrero, "for it will never do to leave him here." At this remove, one feels here a greater anguish and a greater resonance in these spare words than in that much more obviously impassioned, urgent lament Cortés was later to send up on the *Noche Triste* when he had to leave behind some of the loot from Montezuma's treasury.

Is it surprising then that there was a speedy and vigorous development of a folklore of capture and captivity? Only by being forcibly taken and held could a civilized white live the existence of nonexistence with the primitives. No thinking white could *choose* this alternative.

This folklore of captivity was infused both in statement and in veiled suggestion with fears of torture, rape, forced Indianization. In oral tradition as in print the newcomers dwelt almost fondly on narratives of sudden attack, the pioneers peacefully dropping seed in their cleared and muddy fields, the red fiends bursting from the dark verges; on the swift swooping up into savage hands—stained with who knew what horrid crimes against nature—of innocent babes and virtuous women; on the trackless retreat through a wilderness that seemed to harbor these savages as it resisted the pursuing whites; on torture at the stake, the white guts being wound and wound and wound about the pole, the flagging captive staggering slowly, ever more slowly. And, near the center of the tradition, the ruthless violation of white womanhood by the blackened savage in the guttering light of the campfire.

Yet, horrible as this is to contemplate, this is not the worst. The worst is this innermost core: that whites, having been captured, should then fail to attempt escape; refuse to return when ransomed; actually consent to penetration; marry into a tribe.

The only other equally horrifying occurrence was to vanish utterly into the huge maw of the wilderness, leaving no single trace, to be thus lost forever to history.

So capture and loss became the terrible fables of America: women like Frances Slocum, who voluntarily lived with the Indians for more than sixty years after her capture, or Mary Jemison, who after more than seventy years with the Shawnee could still speak reverently of them, of the love she bore them; and the vanished, destroyed expeditions and settlements—the Narvaez expedition to Florida in 1527 in the course of which all but a handful of the original six hundred were lost, and Raleigh's "Lost Colony" of Roanoke.

Thus it is neither accident nor mere historical circumstance that made the captivity narrative America's first form of popular literature and allowed it to pass almost simultaneously into the status of a folk genre, complete with its conventions, tale types, motifs. Its peculiar virtues were precisely those that were needed: in its detailed descriptions of savage tortures it reconfirmed the hideous, satanic character of the enemy; in its descriptions of savage life it reconfirmed the immeasurable superiority of civilization; and in the resistance of the captive—for Frances Slocum and Mary Jemison were awful exceptions—whites found the New World equivalent of the old Biblical injunctions (which explains the unvarying use of the term "redeemed" to describe the safe return of captives).

Nor is it accident that the heroes and heroines of American folk legend are those whose resistance was so singular, so bloody, that their stories were endlessly retold. Hannah Dustin was one. She not only resisted and escaped, but went back to kill and scalp her abductors and so claim the bounty their scalps would bring. And the Johnson lads of West Virginia, captured in 1788, had an irresistible tale. By the lurid glow of a campfire these mere children slew their grown male captors and made their way home.

Yet despite the remarkable way in which the captivity narrative served as a concise, complete, symbolic guide to the wilderness and to civilization's mission in it, there was another alternative, another sort of response than this terrible, fierce fear of the wild New World. And this was precisely what Robert Frost in "The Gift Outright" called salvation in surrender, though he was wrong to think this could be achieved through blood spilled, wars fought.

No. White civilization's salvation here in the Americas, its chance for a spiritual regeneration through the confrontation with newness, would have been to accept and understand the Indians: to appreciate their unique, often beautiful adjustments to their lands of living. And regeneration might also have come through a selective borrowing of aboriginal cultural traits, especially habits of mind, most especially that crucial humility before the vast space of the continents, and a sense of the fragile interconnectedness of all life. Furthermore, a mingling of the races might in time have produced a truly new race considerably unlike the one that Crèvecoeur and countless others never tired of claiming we already were.

In fact, examples of such mingling do exist, not in folklore but in history. They exist in the captivity tradition, and in those dread, cautionary tales of vanished expeditions.

Cabeza de Vaca, one of the four survivors of that fantastically bungled Narváez expedition of 1527, wrote what might be the first New World captivity narrative. In it he told in sparse words of survival during eight years of wandering, and of slavery and starvation among the tribes of the Gulf Coast. And yet well as such a narrative might have served white ends, it seems clear that de Vaca's redemption occurred some time *before* he re-emerged into the light of civilization in 1536. You have to look carefully for it in his *Relación* addressed to "His Sacred Caesarian Majesty," Charles V. But it is there, as Haniel Long divined it in his interlinear companion to the *Relación*. For this man and his companions survived that eight years sojourn by transforming themselves from conquistadores into healers. They started out indiscriminately murdering the natives and laying waste the landscape, and were reduced at last to eating the putrescent corpses of their own dead. Later, however, the men moved among the tribes as life-bringers, life-enhancers. And once they had accomplished this transformation, the closed thickets and dense marshlands of the wilderness opened as if by magic. The whole country opened, revealing to their startled eyes complete tribes singing their praises, dancing their arrivals and departures. Unwittingly and perhaps even against conscious intention, de Vaca and his companions had tapped the uncharted spiritual reservoir of the New World, insuring their way through what would otherwise have been impenetrable hostility. Where once they would have been met by arrows, now they were greeted with offerings of food.

And so, by the time de Vaca and his companions re-emerged out of the interior darkness of the wilderness into the light of *Nueva España*, they had become convinced of something few of their countrymen would have been prepared to see: that the Indians like the whites were children of one Great Spirit. Not many years after this the Spaniards would hold a full-dress debate at the royal court at Valladolid where this proposition was actually the issue, though as Lewis Hanke writes in his account of that remarkable cultural phenomenon, a decision was never rendered. Here in America in 1536 such a notion of spiritual brotherhood could not even have been a question, for as de Vaca and the others stepped out of the woods they saw their countrymen at their accustomed work, driving a slave coffle through a ruined landscape that had once been home.

Then, too, beneath the bones of the legend of Raleigh's Lost Colony, still popularly assumed to have been butchered to the last infant by Powhatan's savage henchmen, we can also glimpse what might have been.

When Governor John White finally returned to the forbidding coasts of Roanoke Island in 1590, three years after having gone back to England for supplies, he ordered a trumpet sounded across the water to the island in the agreed-upon signal. But its tinny echo went lonely and unanswered. Some English airs were then struck up on deck, their foreign sounds sent toward the only bit of land on that whole, huge coastline where they could hope to strike familiar ears. Nothing.

When they finally could get ashore through the heavy swell, they found the sure signs of destruction, desolation: an empty palisade, discarded boxes and cases, muskets with their locks rusted into inutility, books busted open and swollen as if infected by the land with some fatal disease. Nothing else but the deeply incised letters on the palisade: CROATOAN.

But on that nearby spit, there was nothing, either, and now the full, horrid gloom of the wilderness seemed to swoop down about the searchers: the wilderness, its savage inhabitants, had swallowed whole and without trace this entire colony of civilization. Sickened and terrified by this, White weighed anchor and turned his back on such a land, and at that moment the Lost Colony entered legend as one of those grim, cautionary tales that powerfully conditioned succeeding efforts at settlement.

Yet now it is incontrovertibly established that these whites were not massacred but that instead they joined their friends, the Hatteras (or Croatan) Indians, and with them migrated steadily inland until at last they really were lost to white recall. Over the years as the legend grew and darkened, expeditions were sent out fruitlessly again and again to discover some least trace and so recover these civilized people to history. Finally, in the early eighteenth century when Scottish immigrants and French Hugenots began pushing into the interior of North Carolina, they found there, living in log cabins and tilling the soil, a peaceful, mixed-blood race which traced its lineage back to the coastlands and to the mingling of the English and the Hatteras. But still that possibility, that buried alternative, could not be accepted. Regarding these people, John Lawson, North Carolina's pioneer historian, wrote that this was the mongrelized remains of

> a settlement that miscarried for want of timely supplies from England; or through the treachery of the natives, for we may reasonably suppose that the English were forced to cohabit with them for relief and conservation; and that in the process of time they conformed themselves to the manners of their Indian relations; and thus we see how apt human nature is to degenerate.

Their descendants are still there in what is now Robeson County, but the moral their history contains has as yet to be assimilated by their white neighbors.

A 1722 version of a beaver

Nor was the true meaning exhumed from the facts beneath the legend of Frances Slocum, the "Lost Sister of Wyoming." She was kidnapped by the Delaware Indians in 1778 and was discovered living contentedly with the Miami tribe in Indiana Territory in 1835. Once her surviving brothers learned of her whereabouts, they hastened out to the territory to redeem the long-held captive.

They found the squalid settlement, as they would have to have regarded it, and within it the cabin where their sister lived. But one of the brothers recorded the deep shock that went through them all when they looked again upon the face of their blood kin: a face seamed and darkened by a lifetime out of doors. Oh, God! said one, gazing upon this. Is *this* my sister?

And yet, shocked as they were at her appearance, the rude neatness of her quarters, the terrific strangeness of those dark relatives who moved about her, still more shaken were they when they learned—as they very soon did—that the Lost Sister in no way considered herself lost and refused to return with them to civilization. These were her people, she told them, and if she were to die in civilization, the Great Spirit would not know where to find her.

What a sensation her story then raised among the whites! A spate of pamphlets and books appeared, dwelling upon her tragedy. A special act of Congress exempted her from deportation with the rest of her people to the western shores of the Mississippi. Even the President, William Henry Harrison, became interested in her "case."

All of which obscured the hard but simple truth that this woman, like Mary Jemison, Caty Sage, Cynthia Ann Parker, and uncounted others, most definitely did not regard herself, or her story, as tragic. Her life with the Indians had been a fulfilling one, and she made very clear how deeply she loved her husband, their children and relations, and her people—the Miami. Only when her white relations began to meddle, as they had to, did she begin to regret her condition. And at last, robbed of her fellow tribespeople, a lonely, isolated cultural freak in the midst of a new white settlement, she settled into her terminal illness. She steadfastly refused white medical aid, saying that her people had all gone away, and now she wished to go also.

She was betrayed, of course, by a Christian burial, nor could they allow her to sleep peacefully thereafter. More than seventy years after her death, her kinsman, Charles E. Slocum, M.D., LL.B., PH.D., stood before a meeting of the American Association for the Advancement of Science and argued that Frances' Christian background, her white blood, had protected her throughout her long captivity as with an impermeable shield. She was really always white.

Cabeza de Vaca and his companions, the members of the Lost Colony, and Frances Slocum are not, as I have said, isolated examples of this alternative to fear and fierce resistance: there are literally hundreds of such examples, though often these lie buried in out-of-the-way places, and many no doubt were totally unrecorded. But those we do have constitute one of the most remarkable and deeply interesting aspects of New World history. They must stand for the many, many lives lived silently with the tribes and in an intense relationship with the new lands. Standing for this, they can also speak to us of what should have been the American Dream: that of spiritual regeneration here in these vast, untamed lands, through learning to value differences, accepting our own limitations as well as those of others, and by marrying ourselves to an environment we have yet to learn to live with.

This thoughtful, provocative article has been excerpted from Frederick Turner's forthcoming book, The Cost of Living, *to be published this spring by The Godine Press. Mr. Turner is editor of* The North American Indian Reader *and* Geronimo.

Barney Oldfield

"Who the hell do you think you are—Barney Oldfield?" That was the motorcycle cop's standard question for fifty years, and even today you can hear it once in a while if you get caught speeding. For Oldfield's name still holds the dim thunder of the huge, primitive racing cars that slammed through the dust at the murderous dirt-track meets of the turn of the century. Barney Oldfield was not the best driver in that reckless era; his rival, Ralph De Palma, for instance, handled a car better. But of all the early racing men, only Oldfield became legendary. No cop ever asked, "Who the hell do you think you are—Ralph De Palma?"

Berna Eli Oldfield was born on an Ohio farm in 1878. Like many of the boys who were growing up in the 1890's, he became infected with the cycling craze, and he began his racing career on a borrowed Royal Flush bicycle in an 1894 cross-country contest. He came in second. Two years later he was barnstorming through the Midwest with his Racycle Racing Team, billing himself as "The Bicycle Champion of Ohio."

Oldfield was shifting his allegiance to motorcycles by 1902, when he received a letter from an old cyclist friend named Tom Cooper. Cooper had recently abandoned the sport to help a mechanic named Henry Ford—who was trying to grub up enough money to start a motor company—build a pair of racing cars. The cars were taking shape, and Cooper wanted Barney to come to Detroit and lend a hand.

Cooper was supposed to be Ford's driver, but in fact no one was anxious to handle the cars. They were nothing but engine and frame, steered by handle bars, with exposed crankshafts that sprayed oil over the driver. Oldfield was enchanted by them. He begged for a chance to try one, was given the "999" (named after the New York Central's famous locomotive), and took it around the mile-long Grosse Point track in slightly over a minute. He was immediately chosen to drive in an upcoming race against the champion Alexander Winton in his favored car, the Bullet. "Well," Oldfield's biographer William Nolan quotes the fledgling driver as saying, "this damn chariot may kill me, but they will say afterward that I was goin' like hell when she took me over the bank!" And sure enough, to the astonishment of everyone but Oldfield, the Ohio cyclist boomed past Winton's machine to win the five-mile race.

The ensuing publicity got Ford the financial backing to start his company. It also launched Oldfield's career. The next spring he rammed the 999 around a mile track in 59 and 3/5 seconds, becoming the first man in America to drive a gas-powered car a mile a minute. A month later he shaved four seconds off his record. As *The Automobile* magazine told it: ". . . Oldfield with a roar like unto a passing comet, skidded around the far turn and flashed past the howling, horn-tooting crowd . . . in an exhibition that caused the whole great crowd to gulp and gasp. Men were white-faced and breathless, while women covered their eyes. . . . When the judges hung out 55⁴/5 seconds as the time the riot of sound broke loose afresh."

In the years that followed, Oldfield became a national figure. He drove throughout the country in cars with wonderful names—the Green Dragon, the Golden Submarine, the Killer Christie, the Blitzen Benz. The automobiles were heavy, overpowered monsters with thin, unreliable tires, and Oldfield had his share of accidents. He chipped his teeth in one, and thereafter drove with a cigar clenched in his mouth to check the vibrations. The cheroot became his most enduring trademark.

He made a great deal of money in those days, but always spent it faster than it came in. He was arrogant, boastful, and he drank. His friend the prize fighter Jim Jeffries said, "I did more fighting in saloons getting old Barney out of scrapes than I ever did in the ring." Once, Oldfield showed up at a track with a hangover so blinding that he drove his car through the fence on the first turn.

But his popularity remained strong. In 1910 he set a new world speed record of 131.7 miles per hour in the big, chain-driven Blitzen Benz, and left this rich description of the run: "I let the great machine have its head, and for fully a third of the distance the wheels were off the ground while I fought for control. The front wheels were shooting up and down in a weird dance, and I knew that if a tire burst I would be beyond mortal help. I shot through space until . . . I approached the verge of unconsciousness. Then I shut her down, knowing I had traveled faster than any other human on earth." Kaiser Wilhelm sent him a personal telegram: I CONGRATULATE A DARING YANKEE ON SO REMARKABLE A PERFORMANCE IN A GERMAN CAR.

Shortly after this triumph, however, he was suspended from events sanctioned by the American Automobile Association after he had defied the organization to run a ludicrous race against Jack Johnson, a fine prize fighter but an inept driver. Cut off from the big races, he kept before the public by barnstorming country fairs with two other drivers who would always ease off at the last minute so that the fans could see their hero win a split-second victory.

Oldfield was eventually readmitted to the AAA. He still drove hard, and he often won races. But he was slowing down. Finally, in 1918, he retired.

His happiest days were behind him now. He promoted Firestone tires for a while, but he drank too much, and the job was gently taken away from him. He lost all his money in the stock market, went through a succession of stormy marriages, and, ironically, spent some time giving lectures on auto safety for the Plymouth Motor Corporation. He took to hanging around in bars, cornering customers and asking forlorn questions: Did they remember when he crashed at Corona in 1913? Did they remember when he won the 1914 Cactus Derby? They almost never did.

Barney Oldfield died in 1946 of a cerebral hemorrhage. It was not the end he would have chosen. "If I go," he had once said, "I want it to be in the Blitzen Benz, or a faster car if they ever build one, with my foot holding the throttle wide open. I want the grandstand to be crowded and the band playing the latest rag. I want them all to say, as they file out the gate, 'Well, old Barney—he was goin' some!'"

by Richard F. Snow

THE TVA:

IT AIN'T WHAT IT USED TO BE

What has befallen "the greatest peacetime achievement of twentieth-century America" since the New Deal

by James Branscome

I n recent years, as the energy crisis has developed, and bureaucracies in Washington have wrestled with little success to solve it, and Congress has moved slower than a West Virginia coal train even to agree on a battle strategy, some Americans have proposed that a public agency based in Knoxville, Tennessee, become the model for coping with the problem.

On first impression Knoxville seems an unlikely site for providing a solution to an internationally baffling crisis. For three decades the civic fathers of that eastern Tennessee center have smarted over John Gunther's pronouncement that it was probably the ugliest city he had seen inside America. Whatever the demerits of the Knoxville skyline, its two tallest and newest structures in 1976 were the headquarters for the Tennessee Valley Authority (TVA), a New Deal-era agency that once made the city the dateline for any discussion of public ownership, resource management, or the success of F.D.R.'s depression-recovery program. No fewer than sixty-five heads of state, most of them from developing nations, have made a visit to TVA a necessary part of surveying America, and many have returned home to imitate the workings of the agency that TVA supporters now propose extending to a larger area of the United States to take on the energy crisis.

Though TVA's national profile receded after it won the last of its major political survival battles in the 1950's, its continuing work in the seven-state Tennessee River Valley area transformed it into the nation's largest utility, the near single source of new ideas for chemical fertilizer development, and a growing fountain of suggestions on how to manage the nation's resources without dragging the afterbirth of bureaucracy into all dealings with people as an accompaniment. At a time when electric bills nationally exceeded mortgage payments in some cases for the middle class, and welfare payments for some of the poor, TVA's ability to produce power at rates 45 per cent below the national average made its virtues even more appealing.

Senator Adlai E. Stevenson of Illinois introduced a bill in Congress to create a Federal Oil and Gas Corporation, based on the TVA organizational model, to compete with the oil industry in drilling on federal lands, inland and off-shore, and selling oil and gas to refineries. Senators Edward M. Kennedy of Massachusetts and George McGovern of South Dakota, Lee White, a former chairman of the Federal Power Commission, Leonard Woodcock, president of the United Auto Workers, and consumer advocate Ralph Nader, among others, supported the measure. Former Oklahoma Senator Fred Harris suggested using TVA as a model in reforming private utilities. Seconding him were groups like the National Coalition for Land Reform, and consumer organizations in various parts of the country who were seeking relief from power prices.

Ironically, however, while national leaders were re-discovering TVA, grassroots elements across TVA's 80,000-square-mile area were revolting against it. Farmers, ratepayers, strip-mined land owners, coal suppliers, unions, and politicians in Tennessee, Alabama, Mississippi, Kentucky, Virginia, North Carolina, and Georgia, loaded down visiting reporters with reams of TVA critiques full of quotes honed for printing. The agency seemed almost under siege by this new brand of opposition, and so mystified by its volume that its historic proficiency at persuasion was replaced by dump loads of defensive press releases issued from its Knoxville headquarters. TVA is accustomed to battling. What was different in the mid-1970's was that it was dueling not with outside power interests, but with its own people. TVA's chief information officer, who commanded a public relations and technical information budget of $1.3 million, called the criticism "healthy," and then sighed, "I hope."

When President Franklin D. Roosevelt leaned back in his chair on May 18, 1933, and handed Senator George W. Norris of Nebraska the pen with which he had just signed the TVA act, he could not have guessed that he had just launched the most enduringly controversial program of the New Deal. It was true that the bill the President signed was the 138th that had been introduced in Congress

since 1921 relating to the disposition of the Tennessee Valley. The new act resembled bills vetoed in 1928 by President Calvin Coolidge and in 1931 by President Herbert Hoover, but Roosevelt hoped that he had laid to rest national socialism and regional favoritism debates with the promise that TVA would be "a corporation clothed with the power of Government but possessed of the flexibility and initiative of a private enterprise," and concerned with the Tennessee River Valley but working "for the general social and economic welfare of the Nation."

For all the comfort those words gave the private power interests, Roosevelt might as well have said that he was creating a socialist river-damming project that would be used to barge children to integrated schools and supply electric power to the Kremlin. Words like a "yardstick" by which true power costs could be judged, and multipurpose "planning," were signals to the program's opponents that what the liberal New York Democrat and Norris, the progressive Nebraska Republican, had in mind was more than another public relief program for the eroded hills and pocketbooks of the Southern mountaineer and his flatland neighbors who lived farther down the flood-prone Tennessee River.

While the New Deal "Brain Trust" was frequently given credit for the TVA idea, proposals to uplift the Tennessee River Valley went all the way back to John Calhoun's proposal to President James Monroe in 1824 to appropriate funds to remove the river blockage at Muscle Shoals, Alabama. Other proponents of national development took up similar proposals in later generations, but not until the end of the nineteenth century were the basic theoretical premises of TVA formulated. It was Gifford Pinchot, chief forestry adviser to President Theodore Roosevelt and a leading spokesman for the conservation movement, who first elaborated what was to become the major theme of TVA-style regional development. "A river," said Pinchot, "is essentially a unit from its source to the sea" and should be harnessed for "all the uses of the waters and the benefits to be derived from their control."

Pinchot's definition of conservation as "the use of the earth for the good of man"—with emphasis on how a young nation was squandering its vast resources—built the consciousness that eventually created TVA and sustained its first officials. On its twentieth anniversary TVA used Pinchot's definition as an epigraph for its annual report to the President and Congress, and cited TVA's achievements as a tribute to the soundness of his ideas. The TVA founders believed that they had created a unique government agency which met President Theodore Roosevelt's criticism of our national development policy as "the piecemeal execution of projects," without a planned responsibility that is "definitely laid on one man or group of men who can be held accountable."

Not until 1917 were any facilities other than marginally useful canals built at Muscle Shoals. That year the government announced that it had chosen the Shoals area as a site for the wartime production of nitrates for munitions so that the U.S. could reduce its dependence on Chile for its supply. The nitrate plant was not completed until January,

PRECEDING PAGE: *Soaring a thousand feet, the twin stacks of TVA's giant coal-fired steam plant at Cumberland City, Tennessee, symbolize TVA power. The plant can generate 2,600,000 kilowatts.*

1919, and the dam—named Wilson Dam, after the President—that was to supply its power was delayed in final construction until 1925. In 1921 the Secretary of War had asked for bids on the Muscle Shoals facilities in accordance with the routine disposal of government "surplus property." One of the bidders, in what became one of the most talked-about stories of the early 1920's, was Henry Ford. The auto magnate magnanimously offered $5 million for the government's $90 million investment. He promised a Ruhr Valley in the American southland that sent real estate speculators scurrying to the area. Fate was against Ford, however, whose bid was not accepted even after he made a highly publicized trip to Muscle Shoals in the company of Thomas Edison.

Somehow, the bills to dispose of Muscle Shoals landed in the Senate's Agriculture Committee chaired by Senator Norris rather than in the Military Affairs Committee, where they might have been expected to be sent. "I never have known how it came to be dumped upon my lap," Norris wrote in his autobiography, *Fighting Liberal.* But "after beating back efforts of private interests to get Muscle Shoals," he launched an intensive battle to create TVA, only to have his bills vetoed twice. Behind Norris' motivation was his well-known antipathy for the "well-intrenched, enormously rich, and powerful forces" he felt controlled the nation. In TVA he saw, "not daring to express it publicly . . . a model by which this country could see the happiness, material progress, and prosperity to be attained if the American people act promptly and properly in the preservation of God-given natural resources of the country."

Presidential candidate Franklin D. Roosevelt, who had fought high utility rates as governor of New York, endorsed the Norris bill, and as President-elect demonstrated his interest in TVA by visiting Muscle Shoals. On April 10, 1933—during the famous first hundred days of his administration—he sent the Congress a message asking for the creation of TVA, promising that the new authority would be a "return to the spirit and vision of the pioneer. If we are successful here," he said, "we can march on, step by step, in the like development of other great national territorial units within our borders." By May 18, 1933, he had signed the bill "for the especial purpose of bringing about in said Tennessee drainage basin and adjoining territory . . . the maximum amount of flood control; the maximum development . . . for navigation purposes; the maximum generation of electric power consistent with flood control and navigation; the proper use of marginal lands; the proper method of reforestation . . . and the economic and social well-being of the people living in said river basin; and to provide for the national defense."

For a government agency the act allowed a very flexible program. Other than the general development mandate, the act's most explicit requirements were that the new authority—in fact, a government corporation—would be ruled by three presidentially appointed directors, one to be designated chairman, who would serve for nine-year terms with the consent of the Senate. The act dictated that the agency locate its headquarters in the region, excluded it from Civil Service laws, and required the three directors to believe in the "feasibility and wisdom of the Act." The directors would report to the President, consult Congress on appropriations not covered by power revenues, and otherwise be free to develop the "model" that Norris and Roosevelt wanted to spill across the American landscape. Depending on the point of view of the observer, the power of the board of directors of TVA was either the most ideal arrangement ever devised by government for grassroots input, allowing three men to bend to the demands of their constituencies and the wiles of a river; or it was the first Washington-imposed dictatorship that blanketed an entire region. No one at the time of TVA's creation or since has doubted that the validity of either of these views depends on the caliber and character of the three directors.

For chairman of TVA, Roosevelt chose Arthur E. Morgan, the president of Antioch College in Ohio, who had a national reputation as the hydraulic engineer who had tamed the Miami River after it had visited a disastrous flood on the city of Dayton. From his experience in resisting political appointees to the board of the Miami Conservancy District, Morgan had learned to be suspicious of politicians. Though Roosevelt promised him "there is to be no politics in this," Morgan came to have doubts, believing that Roosevelt "worked out a philosophy that made ethical considerations secondary to the possession of power." That statement hinted at the righteousness with which Morgan regarded public service, how he believed human frailties could profit from the discipline of engineering, and how his moralism would eventually conflict with TVA's

The Fontana Dam, TVA's highest (480 feet), was built during World War II on the Little Tennessee River in North Carolina.

The first board of directors of TVA comprised three distinguished men who were not altogether compatible in their views of the agency. Arthur E. Morgan (far left), the chairman, was an idealist who wanted to apply principles of hydraulic engineering to human uplift; Harcourt A. Morgan (center; no relation) was interested above all in TVA's fertilizer program; David Lilienthal—later chairman of the Atomic Energy Commission—focused primarily on the efficient production of electric power.

directors and Roosevelt in a way that almost wrecked the agency.

The President told Morgan to choose his two colleagues on the board, taking care that one be familiar with power development and the other with Southern agriculture. The chairman first chose Dr. Harcourt A. Morgan (no relation), the president of the University of Tennessee, a Canadian-born entomologist who had advanced rapidly in the hierarchy of the Southern land-grant college system because of his research on the boll weevil. Supreme Court Justice Louis Brandeis, a friend of Chairman Morgan's, then suggested a young Wisconsin attorney named David Lilienthal for the third directorship. Brandeis had heard good reports of Lilienthal's performance on the Wisconsin Public Service Commission.

From their first meeting, the three directors were considerably at odds. On that occasion Chairman Morgan presented a letter from Wendell L. Willkie, president of Commonwealth and Southern Corporation, who wanted to know just how TVA would function as a "yardstick." Morgan was willing to exchange ideas with Willkie in a spirit of honest competition, an attitude that alarmed Lilienthal. Time thereafter quickly proved that personalities and personal philosophies could become—however petty they were—major obstacles in even the most revolutionary of agencies. H. A. Morgan, it turned out, was far more interested in fertilizer programs than in social revolution. Lilienthal, while a reformer at heart, was a practical politician who believed the power program was the major ingredient that would revolutionize the valley. The chairman thought a cautious approach to the power program would allow concentration on uplifting the human resources of the region.

Given this background of discord, which lasted until the chairman was removed by Roosevelt in 1938, the achievements of the first board of directors were remarkable. To build Norris Dam—its first—the board dispensed with private contractors and hired its own construction forces, a policy that still continues. The workers were recruited without the patronage that dominated other New Deal programs, were trained for their jobs, allowed to bargain collectively with the agency, and provided with housing, libraries, and cultural activities. Rates charged by TVA-organized cooperative distributors allowed regional use to attain that of double the national average and forced the competing private companies in the South to lower their rates by nearly one half. Through the extension services of the Agriculture Department the agency enlisted, in five years, more than twenty-three thousand farmers in its demonstration fertilizer programs. Its nurseries turned out sixty-one million seedlings for forestry development. It completed three dams and was working on four more in 1938. Agency efforts all but eliminated malaria, an affliction that had affected up to one third of the population in some areas. But, most importantly, it captured the imagination of the people of the Tennessee Valley, won over many of the doubters in the region's conservative establishment, and kept its profile high enough to merit regular attention from Roosevelt and such influential newspapers as the *New York Times.*

Though the early TVA demonstrated unusual sensitivity and courage in certain areas of human concern such as hiring black-listed miners and holding up the flooding of a reservoir because of a bedridden landowner, in other areas it made crucial compromises. Despite Chairman Morgan's claim that blacks were hired in proportion to their percentage in the regional population, there is evidence that even black college graduates were kept in menial jobs. Certainly blacks were housed in segregated areas, and separate toilet and drinking facilities for blacks and whites were installed at all TVA dams. Though Eleanor Roosevelt was a friend of many of the agency's early executives and a major influence on other liberals who flocked to TVA, her efforts on behalf of women were never reflected in their having a major role in the agency. (Even today, of the top thirty-seven staff people who meet with the board each two weeks, only one is a woman and one a black.) The agency all but turned over important parts of its agricultural program under H. A. Morgan's direction to the conservative Extension Service and the American Farm Bureau Federation, which worked mainly with more prosperous farmers.

As tremendously successful as the dams and recreation areas were for flood prevention and economic relief, they were not built without sacrifice. Whole communities were uprooted for reservoirs behind dams, and traditional folkways and community cohesiveness had to make way for a new brand of progress. Since its inception, TVA has forced the removal of 125,480 persons from their homes in a territory slightly larger than New England. Most of the removal occurred during the early years when dams were being built "by assembly-line methods," as one executive described it. To tame the Tennessee River TVA created what Donald Davidson, the Vanderbilt University writer, called a two-million-acre "permanent flood."

Though the power program had been only one of many elements of regional development envisioned by the founders, challenge after challenge from private power interests forced it—and Lilienthal as power affairs manager—into the forefront of national attention. The first of many legal hurdles put in the way of TVA came from a coalition of coal and ice companies who claimed that hydro power would threaten coal consumption and replace ice dealers with refrigerators. When courts refused to hear that case, TVA opponents organized a stockholders' suit to prevent the Alabama Power Company from negotiating with the agency over power territory. Known as the *Ashwander* case, it was appealed to the Supreme Court, which upheld TVA. The utilities themselves organized and filed another suit, only to be rebuffed again in the courts. The years of legal challenges delayed important advances in TVA's power program, further divided Lilienthal and the more cautious chairman, and brought Wendell Willkie into the national limelight for his run for the Presidency against Roosevelt in 1940.

Chairman Morgan, increasingly disaffected with his two board colleagues, began to air his grievances in the press. Though rarely specific, he hinted in public statements and magazine articles that the other two members were involved in "evasion, intrigue and sharp strategy," and in "subtle forms of failure to meet a public trust." Pressed by the President and by a congressional investigation, Morgan eventually revealed that his most serious reservation about his colleagues concerned what he saw as their connivance in a move by private interests to secure mineral rights on land that was part of the Norris Dam site. But the chairman pro-

duced no evidence—before or after his removal by the President—that his colleagues had acted unprofessionally or illegally in this or other matters. In finally removing Morgan, the President told Congress "he is temperamentally unfitted to exercise a divided authority."

Until his death in 1975, Arthur Morgan continued to provide ammunition for a debate over whether Lilienthal had destroyed the TVA ideal by limiting it to a narrowly defined agency concerned almost entirely with being a utility. Lilienthal supporters had ample volumes of his writings on which to base a case that Morgan was an eccentric and politically naive engineer trying to apply hydrology principles to the vagaries of human character. Both men's genius had made TVA more than just another federal pork barrel; but their pettiness raised serious doubts that it was a national "model."

Roosevelt named H. A. Morgan chairman in 1938 and Lilienthal chairman in 1941. It was Lilienthal's leadership in the power program during World War II that made TVA a major contributor to national defense. In 1941, before U.S. entry in the war, the Office of Production Management asked TVA to increase its capacity by 100,000 kilowatts of power to enable the expansion of aluminum production for bombers. OPM gave the agency a timetable calling for the new capacity by the winter of 1943, and TVA engineers determined that they could build a required new dam on the French Broad River within that time. At the behest of landowners who would be flooded out, however, Senator Kenneth McKellar of Tennessee, the ranking member of the Senate Committee on Appropriations, held up construction, suggesting other dam sites. Standing by Lilienthal's principle that "experts as well as rivers have no politics," the engineers refused to accept alternative locations. After the attack on Pearl Harbor, President Roosevelt got a congressional go-ahead, and the engineers

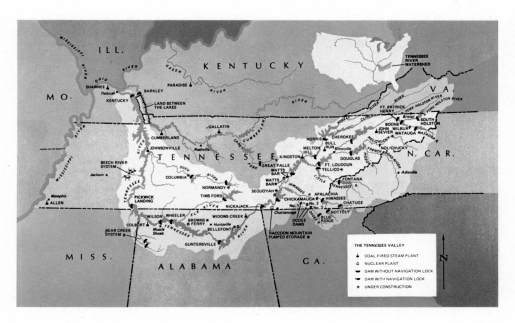

This recent TVA map illustrates the tremendous extent and variety of the agency's installations.

Before TVA: primitive water resources, heavy land erosion, and frequent floods—all greatly alleviated by the agency's programs

decades TVA had tamed the river, established a power territory and system, rebuilt the region's eroded hills, and fulfilled Roosevelt's hope for an agency that "touches and gives life to all forms of human concerns."

Following the river system plan devised by Arthur Morgan, the agency had proved that a river could be harnessed for flood control, power generation, navigation, and human uplift all at once—an idea that used to keep the Army Corps of Engineers in stitches over predicted fumblings of the maverick engineer. Thanks to Lilienthal, the agency had won the battle for public power, proving in the process the contested notion that a heavy electrical load and not consumer subsidy of transmission lines was the way to get volume power to neglected rural customers at the lowest price. The debatable conservative approach of TVA's agriculture programs notwithstanding, H. A. Morgan's efforts with fertilizers and farmers laid the groundwork for the restoration of valley farms and the chemical secrets of the processes that later produced the international "green revolution." Altogether it was a remarkable record, doubly so because of its experimental nature and the political odds stacked against it.

In twenty years the agency had built twenty dams on the nation's fifth largest river, turning the 650-mile unpredictable and destructive giant into the nation's most controlled river. At that time the total dam system had cost over $25 million and averted potential flood damage of more than $51 million. In 1952 alone the navigation system had saved barge shippers $10 million at an expense of $3.5 million to the government. Since 1933 the agency had reforested 212,000 acres of land and produced 295 million seedlings in its nursery. Over the same period sixty-eight thousand farmers had allowed their farms to be TVA test demonstration areas to educate them and their neighbors about new farming techniques. Per capita income had risen from 44 per cent of the national average in 1929 to 61 per cent in 1952. Manufacturing employment opportunities had increased 57 per cent faster in the valley than in the nation.

As impressive as the statistics were, they failed to convey the sheer magnitude of the project in the seven-state area of 201 counties. The concrete, rock, and earth laid in the path of the river and its tributaries was twelve times the bulk of the Great Pyramids. The volume of water behind its dams could cover the entire state of Illinois to a depth of eight inches. The construction effort at its peak in World War II had required forty-two thousand employees. But more importantly—and surprisingly—an agency that had had a vague mandate to "sell the surplus power not used in its operations" had by its twentieth year become the nation's largest utility, selling power at the lowest possible prices to a people who in 1933 had had almost no knowledge of the electric age. By 1953 the agency's customers were consuming twice as much power as their national counterparts.

TVA had also become a government organization that the valley's people believed they could trust. When the private power companies built "spite lines" to claim TVA power territory, farmers chopped down the poles. John Gunther reported on his trek through the region that

set up a "hot line" phone system from Washington to the dam site so that work could begin the moment the President's pen left the authorizing bill. The agency then completed the dam in thirteen months, setting a new world record for construction speed. Unbeknownst to TVA—although Lilienthal had some privy information—its power would also meet a critical need for the production of the atomic bomb at nearby Oak Ridge. With its power capacity and its production of munitions at Muscle Shoals, TVA's significant role in the war ultimately helped to silence a large number of its critics.

By the end of 1953 the agency had reached many of its original goals. In some respects all that was to happen after that date were finishing touches. While its later accomplishments were still extraordinary, by the end of the first two

TVA's employees were the most fiercely loyal group he had ever encountered. Thanks to the abilities and connections of Chairmen Morgan and Lilienthal and to favorable newspaper coverage, the TVA story was internationally well known, and the nation's liberal community stood ready to defend the agency against its detractors. In 1950 historian Henry Steele Commager, in common with most academicians, pronounced the agency "the greatest peacetime achievement of twentieth-century America." To win its battles in its third decade, the agency had to cash in those liberal chips.

By the late 1940's TVA engineers had determined that the agency had exhausted most of the hydro power potential of the river and that it would have to turn to steam generation if it was to meet the growing demand on the system coming particularly from the Atomic Energy Commission plants at Oak Ridge and at Paducah, Kentucky. Lilienthal's successor as chairman in 1946, Gordon Clapp, began construction of seven coal-fired plants between 1949 and 1953. In typical TVA fashion, several of them at the time were the world's largest. In 1952 TVA asked the Bureau of the Budget to approve funds for a steam plant north of Memphis on the Mississippi River to supply an anticipated critical need for power in the Memphis area. The proposed new plant, at Fulton, Tennessee, was vigorously opposed by Middle South Utilities' President Edgar Dixon, who feared that a TVA steam plant close to his subsidiaries, Arkansas Power & Light and Mississippi Power & Light, would signal the start of competition from a new TVA power system expansion. The Truman administration in its final days approved the capacity increase for the agency, but Congress waited on a budget request from the incoming Eisenhower administration before voting the necessary appropriations.

Eisenhower's budget left out the Fulton plant, and the new President let Congress know his antagonism to TVA by labeling it an example of "creeping socialism" and accusing the agency of stealing industries from other areas. TVA supporters could marshal facts to dispute both claims, but the "socialism" charge by a popular President in 1953 was hard to overcome. That year Eisenhower told his Cabinet, "By God, if ever we could do it, before we leave here, I'd like to see us *sell* the whole thing, but I suppose we can't go that far." The Eisenhower administration was prepared to make good on the President's hope, however, and it set about to cripple TVA's progress.

The administration ploy became known as the Dixon-Yates case, named for Dixon of Middle South Utilities and Eugene Yates of the Southern Company, another power combine. To obviate TVA's need for the Fulton plant, the administration proposed to supply AEC with power from a new privately built Dixon-Yates plant. The controversial plan was advancing until it was discovered in 1955 that the administration had deceptively hidden the fact that the government adviser who had helped devise the plan worked for the financial institution backing the deal. Not even the public outcry over that revelation would have stopped the plan, however, had the city of Memphis not decided to build its own steam plant and ignore the federal government.

When Clapp's term on the board ended, the President named a retiring general of the Corps of Engineers, Herbert Vogel, as chairman, hoping apparently that he could pull the Dixon-Yates deal through. He was unable to do so, and though the administration continued to take pot shots at the agency, the only substantial change in the TVA act came in 1959 when Congress passed an amendment requiring new TVA power program costs to be financed from bonds. It also directed the agency to accelerate its repayment schedules to the U.S. Treasury so that public investment in the power system would be repaid more quickly than originally provided. With the demise of the Dixon-Yates plan, TVA won its last survival struggle, and in the absence of life-and-death controversy its national profile declined.

During the deceptively quiet period after Dixon-Yates, however, another major crisis was developing for the agency. TVA's size, its power, its sometimes lackluster leadership, and its mistakes were cumulatively brewing a series of confrontations with its own people in the valley. The agency that had fought valiantly for conservation and the opportunity for grassroots participation was finding itself up against a new generation of critics with new definitions of conservation and new ways of thinking about participation. In most recent years the confrontations have grown to a crescendo from a disparate chorus of critics.

TVA has been attacked, for instance, by Al Puckett, a representative of Kentucky farmers who claimed that sulfur dioxide from the agency's coal-fired steam plants "defoliated" their crops and that TVA refused to recompense for damages for four years; by Corrine Whitehead, a landowner forced out of TVA's Land Between the Lakes recreation area, who was outraged that the agency was selling lumber from the preserve to the Peabody Coal Company for mine timbers; by Mart Shepherd, a Kentucky landowner whose home used to have a safe water supply and good farm land before a TVA-contracted coal strip-mine company changed all that, with Shepherd picking up the tab; by Arnold Miller, president of the United Mine Workers, who called TVA a "public menace" for buying coal from unsafe and nonunion deep mines and for creating a "nightmare" in Appalachia by purchasing strip-mined coal; by coal operators like Cloyd McDowell of the National Independent Coal Operators Association who charged that TVA gave cost-plus contracts to its conglomerate suppliers, but bid coal down by "predatory purchasing practices" so that small firms had to cut corners or go out of business; by newspapers like the respected Louisville *Courier Journal*, which asked editorially, "Is the TVA Just Another Power Firm?" and answered close to an affirmative; by Tennessee Congressman Joe L. Evins, who claimed that TVA had not done anything about "price gouging" by its coal suppliers; and, finally, by Mrs. Betty Higginbotham of Cleveland, Tennessee, a senior citizen who collected over fifteen thousand signatures on a petition protesting TVA power-rate increases.

TVA's reply to such critics has been forceful and uncompromising. A new chairman, Aubrey Wagner, argued that TVA alone of utilities in the nation has sought a "balance point" between the "polarized extremes" of environmental demands and ecocide. TVA's problems, he said, exemplify on a large scale a question the nation as a whole has not answered: "How does a people, caught between an expanding population and a shrinking resource base, meet its day-to-day needs and at the same time reasonably ensure its future?"

A lifelong veteran of TVA, an engineer who climbed from the ranks to the top, Wagner has few apologies for TVA's programs. "TVA views electricity as a critical catalyst for bringing about a better quality of life for the people. . . . We believe in the usefulness of electric power not to stimulate growth for growth's sake, but because we know what it has done and what it can do to improve the

TVA has gone in heavily for nuclear power plants. This one, at Browns Ferry, Alabama, came close to disaster in March, 1975.

lives of people everywhere." TVA's resistance to strong strip-mine control, air-pollution regulation, coal-mine health and safety laws, and other concerns pressed by its critics has been based on the "balance" theory, providing "the greatest good for the greatest number of people over the longest time," the 62-year-old chairman has said. He warned that if all of TVA's critics were heeded, the valley and the nation would face "total social and economic disaster before the end of the century" because of power shortages.

TVA's chief argument for its policies—one that has grown increasingly less effective in the region, but one that must seem disarmingly appealing to protesting ratepayers across the nation—is that it is required by law to produce power at the lowest possible rates. That it does. With almost the single exception of the Pacific Northwest, where hydro-generation from that region's rivers still predominates, TVA produces the cheapest power in the nation with the same kind of generators and black coal that other large utilities use. One thousand kilowatt hours of power cost TVA's six and one-half million users about $25 in 1976, compared to $63 in New York City, $46 in Boston, $35 in Atlanta, $31 in Los Angeles, and $30 in St. Louis.

TVA's defense of its behavior galls such agency critics as Harry Caudill, the author of *Night Comes to the Cumberlands* and a well-known Kentucky conservationist and public power advocate, who blames TVA's emphasis on low rates for creating and sustaining the ruinous Appalachian strip-mining industry. "The agency is the very epitome of everything evil in the destruction of nature for gain," Caudill charged. It is a fact that stripped coal is cheap coal. But critics of stripped coal argue that it is deceptively cheap because of the social and economic damages it brings to the people and the land. As the nation's largest purchaser of stripped coal from a concentrated area—72 per cent of all of TVA's coal comes from Kentucky—the agency has to bear a large share of the burden, say its critics, for what the nation now seems agreed has been nothing short of recklessness in the destruction of large parts of eastern Kentucky.

While TVA argues that it not only supervises the stripping but also requires reclamation in its contracts, TVA strip mines look no different, and in many cases look worse, than strip mines that sell to private utilities. As a matter of fact, when the state of Kentucky has cited TVA-contracted companies for violations of state law, TVA inspectors have tended to look the other way, comparisons of the state and TVA inspection records indicate. The fact that TVA in 1974 was secretly considering strip mining coal reserves that it owned on twenty-five thousand acres of the presently unstripped Daniel Boone National Forest in Kentucky, until a newspaper exposed the plan, gave credence to arguments by conservationists that TVA's strip-mine practices reflected a greater concern for cheap coal than they did for setting a higher standard of excellence for utilities. A TVA reclamation director, James Curry, said, "Strip mining is part of the American way." That may be true, observed Caudill, for an agency interested in cheap power and power promotion, but it "remains a mockery of the conservationist vision of George Norris."

TVA believed that the demands on its system left it little choice but to pursue the courses it took. In 1951, 85 per cent of the 3,541,000 kilowatts of power generated by TVA was from hydro capacity. By 1955 the agency's output was 9,400,000 kilowatts (a full half of which went to federal installations like AEC's Oak Ridge and Paducah uranium enrichment plants), with 60 per cent of the total power produced by coal-fired plants. Today its generating capacity is 23.3 million kilowatts, 80 per cent of which comes from twelve steam plants using coal. The agency projects that its capacity will increase to 47 million kilowatts in 1985—a whopping 66 per cent increase in a ten-year span. To generate that power the TVA planned the most massive nuclear construction program of any utility in the nation.

If its plans are fulfilled, TVA will retain its role as the nation's largest power producer and largest consumer of coal, and will become the nation's largest generator of power from nuclear energy. Such TVA critics as the former Federal Energy Administration adviser John Gibbons, who went on to become head of the University of Tennessee Environment Center, charged that the agency grossly overestimated power demand growth and would find itself in a few years with excess capacity and higher-than-average rates. In 1974 the power demand on the system actually declined by 14 per cent, but TVA explained that that aberrance in an otherwise growth-oriented region was due to the recession of the period and to power conservation.

Despite its commitment to selling power at the lowest possible rates, TVA also has not escaped criticism over its rate structure. In fact, the agency sells power on a "cost of service" basis, meaning that larger users pay lower rates than those who use less power. TVA has denied charges that this means that users have an incentive to consume, not conserve. Whatever the agency's protestations to the contrary, however, TVA's rate structure has not changed basically since 1953 when, in a less conservation-minded era, the TVA staff proudly admitted in an agency report that its rates were designed to be "promotional."

TVA has proceeded with the planning and construction of seven nuclear plants—five were in the process of being built or sited in 1976—despite growing evidence that its nuclear-powered electric plants may be costlier than originally estimated. It has also had to contend with nuclear critics in the state where the atom bomb was born. TVA's Sequoyah plant—named for the inventor of the Cherokee alphabet—many months behind schedule in construction, doubled in estimated completion costs. The cost overruns on that plant alone would raise consumer bills by about 2 per cent. Power from other sources to make up for the delayed construction of Sequoyah would raise electric bills by another 5 per cent.

On March 22, 1975, TVA made its first major contribution to the nuclear safety controversy when a fire underneath the control room of its Browns Ferry nuclear plant near Athens, Alabama, knocked out both units of the world's largest nuclear generating facility. According to TVA the fire started when a candle being used by an employee to check for air leaks ignited a sealant on electrical cables that controlled the plant's emergency core-cooling system; the flames then spread to other wiring, knocking out the automatic safeguards designed to prevent a nuclear mishap. Had a major water coolant pipe broken during the critical minutes of the eight-hour fire before TVA operators employed manual core-cooling controls, "We would have been in trouble," said Jack R. Calhoun, TVA's nuclear branch chief.

The trouble, according to nuclear critic David Comey of Business and Professional People for the Public Interest, would have been a "catastrophe"—a melt down of the reactor's core, spreading radiation for hundreds of miles. Comey said only "good luck" saved TVA. TVA immediately discounted such a notion, and launched an intensive press campaign to counter the charges of critics and a suspicious press corps.

When nuclear critics learned that the Browns Ferry plant had already had sixty-five "abnormal occurrences" in its short life—Unit 1 went into operation in August, 1974; Unit 2 in March, 1975—and demanded that the TVA board halt its nuclear construction program, TVA chairman Wagner's only response was that nuclear power was still safer than highway driving. The Browns Ferry accident was not even discussed at the regular board meeting following the occurrence until the issue was raised by the press. At that meeting TVA approved $7 million of further expenditures for the Hartsville Nuclear Plant to be located outside Nashville. It is slated to be the world's largest nuclear plant when completed.

For TVA engineers, the Browns Ferry accident was an ego buster. It was the first major flaw in a record of accomplishment that had gained them international fame. Their hope to have Browns Ferry operational again in a "few months" proved too optimistic, as the start-up date stretched to eighteen months, at a cost to the agency of $10 million a month. They were further embarrassed when the accident became a major item of evidence cited by California nuclear critics in support of a referendum in that state for a moratorium on nuclear plants.

It is the question of accountability, of *how* TVA makes decisions about nuclear power, strip mining, dams, etc., that is at the heart of the region's dissatisfaction with the agency. As previously observed, three men, appointed by the President and confirmed by the Senate for nine-year terms, exercise the full authority of the unusually open-ended TVA act. Not until 1975, when pressure from the press and the public forced them to do so, did the three directors ever hold an open board meeting.

TVA has contended that the structure of the agency allows it to have freedom not allotted to the average plodding bureaucracy. On one occasion, Chairman Wagner cited a noisy showdown with TVA's nuclear critics at the Knoxville headquarters building as a good example of why the agency needs to be free to make decisions unhampered by public service commissions, governors, or a voting electorate. "If we built power plants this way, we'd still be operating by kerosene lamps," he said, after both sides had made emotional speeches for and against TVA's nuclear program.

The authority to pass along rate increases and fuel costs without the scrutiny of the public or some administrative body in the states has become a major source of disillusionment with TVA. Scottsboro, Alabama, attorney Bill Garner, a former assistant attorney general of that state, told a U.S. Senate oversight panel in 1975, "I'm a second class citizen from Alabama . . . because I live in the TVA part of Alabama. If anyone . . . who doesn't live in our area wants to complain about his light bill, he can . . . talk to his State senator . . . . But I have to drive all the way to Washington, D.C." Widespread agreement with Garner's position led Tennessee Governor Ray Blanton, with the support of Governors Wallace of Alabama, Waller of Mississippi, and Carroll of Kentucky, to propose that the TVA board be expanded to include four new members, to be nominated by the governor of each state and confirmed by the Senate. "It seems to me that the citizens of the state of Tennessee should have some input into TVA," Governor Blanton said. He was opposed on that notion, however, by Senator Howard Baker of Tennessee, who argued that TVA was "a national asset rather than a regional institution."

Until 1972, when President Nixon appointed Bill Jenkins, a 38-year-old Rogersville, Tennessee, attorney to the board, no native Tennessean or mountaineer had ever served as a TVA director. Although Jenkins' appointment was widely assailed by strip-mine critics because of his controversial reign as supervisor of strip-mine reclamation in Tennessee, many conservationists came to praise him for his insistence on open board meetings, his opposition to the spiraling costs of TVA nuclear plants, and his hostility to land condemnations by the agency. On matters in which he disagreed with the board majority and the staff, Jenkins admitted that he had to look outside the agency for information and advice because he had no staff available to him. When he sought to get accurate information on the death and injury rates in deep mines which sold coal to TVA, for instance, Jenkins found that TVA had no data, and he had to turn to a friend in the Bureau of Mines for the information.

Part of the agency's problems with the valley's people has been a widespread feeling that reflects lack of faith in its credibility. Kentucky farmer Al Puckett put it bluntly: "Farmers in our area don't trust TVA." J. W. Bradley, the head of Save Our Cumberland Mountains, a Tennessee anti–strip-mining group, charged that the agency's employees "willingly accept loads of rock, mud and slate disguised as coal [from coal suppliers] even though they know they're being defrauded." Video tapes supplied by Bradley's organization showing the practice taking place were sufficiently convincing to a House of Representatives investigative committee for it to demand an explanation from TVA. TVA's general manager, Lynn Seeber, admitted that layer-loading of trucks, as it was called, had

occurred, but blamed sampling techniques. As a result of the charges, sampling devices now probe coal loads at varying points rather than at fixed spots known to the coal companies.

Environmental critics pointed also to Seeber's admission on a witness stand in a federal court that he had changed a staff report critical of TVA's Columbia and Normandy dams because it was "too negative," as further evidence that the agency was more interested in self-protection than public candor. After the Whitesburg, Kentucky, *Mountain Eagle* reported that the TVA private security force was maintaining files on critics of the agency's Tellico Dam project, TVA began charging the newspaper $6.75 an hour for time spent by agency file clerks in supplying information which the paper requested. Citing such unusual actions, United Mine Workers president Arnold Miller told a Senate oversight panel, "I am sorry to say that TVA has not been a friend to us. I am even sorrier to say that I don't think TVA gives a damn."

Seeber replied that he changed the staff assessment of the dams because it said "too much about the 'bad' about the project and not enough about the 'good.'" He defended the information charges to the critical Whitesburg newspaper on the ground that the public should not have to subsidize the furnishing of information that is not directly related to public business. Charges from such critics as Arnold Miller came because the agency had a reputation for being more than an average utility, he said. To critics like Richard Ayres of the National Resources Defense Council, who called TVA a "major obstruction" to the nation's air cleanup program because of its opposition to chemical scrubbers, Seeber cited TVA research discrediting the Environmental Protection Agency's insistence that the costly devices were needed to cleanse sulfur dioxide from TVA smokestacks. As a final rejoinder, Seeber said, "We believe TVA has the largest and most comprehensive program of environmental activities of any power producer in the country—as it should have." In 1976, however, the Supreme Court refused to hear TVA's arguments that it should not have to monitor its sulfur dioxide emissions continuously.

As the debate over public power versus private power bloomed again—as it inevitably seemed destined to do— and as the issues of rates, strip mining, and nuclear power received closer attention, TVA got more scrutiny as a prototype of a national "yardstick." That probing, in time, may answer the question of whether TVA has been, as *Forbes* magazine said, a "yardstick with less than 36 inches," or as Paul Wieck of the *New Republic* observed, "a little off course, maybe, but still a damn sight better than the private power trust." Meanwhile, TVA officials have comforted themselves with a statement by former chairman Gordon Clapp that hangs over almost every executive desk: "TVA is controversial because it is consequential; let it become insignificant to the public interest, an agency of no particular account, and the people will stop arguing about it."

James Branscome, a freelance who is a native of the TVA area, has long covered the agency for regional and national publications.

THE WAY I SEE IT

by BRUCE CATTON

DANIEL KRAMER

Around the beginning of the great Bicentennial year a cartoonist got a nationwide chuckle by drawing a sketch of a limitless, totally empty plain somewhere in the western United States. The only thing visible in the vast expanse of unused land was a historical marker, which read:

"On this spot, on July 4, 1776, absolutely nothing happened."

Coming as it did when everybody was scurrying around desperately trying to find a Revolutionary War thread that could be looped about something in the immediate foreground, this brought forth an amused and tolerant response. It centered attention on one point that tended to be overlooked in all the patriotic fervor: by far the greater part of what we now know as the United States was not in the United States at all when independence was proclaimed. Some of it was under another flag, some of it was under no flag; a great deal of it had never been settled and much of it had not even been explored.

Furthermore, if the soil itself was not then under the brand-new flag, neither were most of the people from whom today's Americans are descended. The overwhelming majority of us would have to confess, if pressed, that in 1776 our ancestors were somewhere east of the Atlantic—or west of the Pacific. I myself cannot find that any of my forebears came to America before the new nation was a full half century old. (There is one chilling thought: some of my people then lived in Hesse-Cassell, and I suppose I may be related to some of those Hessian mercenaries who gave King George such a bad name during the Revolution.)

It must be said, however, that the Bicentennial was observed with as much enthusiasm west of the Appalachians as east. One of the unexpected and deeply gratifying points about the whole observance was the fact that it brought forth an immense number of small, intimate local histories—accounts of the settling and developing of a specific town, or county, or geographic area; nothing of the profound, weighty kind that makes professional historians so stuffy, just the homely little facts that cluster about the birth and growth of the smallest village. For some reason the intense preoccupation with the American past which grew out of the Bicentennial seemed to flourish with especial luxuriance in precisely those areas that had no direct, visible connection with the actual revolution. It is as if a great many people had said: "Well, of course, there wasn't anybody here when the Liberty Bell rang, so we can't write about that; but we can tell how Jacob Wright came up the river by flatboat in 1831 and brought eighty acres of land under cultivation, or how somebody built a grist mill on Cold Creek, or why that settlement over beyond Blue Hill petered out and died along in the 'eighties."

These little local histories are by no means out of the direct path that leads from Independence Hall and Yorktown down to the present. They were not grafted onto anything, nor does anyone need to look at them, smile a superior smile, and say: "Oh, yes. How quaint; and really quite interesting, if you have a taste for that sort of thing." These bits and pieces of hitherto unrecorded history are just as vital a part of the American story as Valley Forge or Saratoga. They are simply the later chapters in a story that was born of dreams and daring and continues down through today by faith and endurance. It began on a village green in Lexington and it continues to what you can see when you look out of your bedroom window.

Which means that the great American story is above all other things a *continued* story. It did not start with us and it will not end with us, and it is our story even though we became Americans only yesterday. The tremendous story of the Revolution gains in meaning every time the most recent American is stirred to weave his own story into it. None of these Bicentennial observances has been wasted.

George Washington's Beautiful Nelly

"Miss Eleanor Custis...has more perfection of expression, of color, of softness, and of firmness of mind than I have ever seen before or conceived consistent with mortality. She is everything that the chisel of Phidias aimed at but could not reach, and the soul beaming through her countenance and glowing in her smile is as superior to her face as mind is to matter."

These extravagant words convey the impression that Nelly Custis, George Washington's step-granddaughter, made on the distinguished architect of colonial America, Benjamin Latrobe, when he visited Mount Vernon in 1796. And he was not alone; the Polish Count Julien Niemcewitz, another guest at the Potomac estate at about the same time, called Nelly one of those celestial figures that nature produces only rarely, and insisted that she played, sang, and drew better than any woman in America "or even in Europe." It is one of the small but touching ironies of history that this dazzling young lady, after a youth of extraordinary privilege and corresponding happiness, spent the latter part of her life as an embittered, unattractive matron in a state of constant complaint.

Nelly was the daughter of Martha Washington's son from her previous marriage. However, the relationship between Nelly and George Washington was like that of father and daughter. Nelly's real father, John Parke Custis, had died of fever after following Washington to Yorktown as a volunteer aide during the final stages of the Revolution. After their father's death, Nelly, then aged two, and her six-month-old brother—who bore the impressive name of George Washington Parke Custis—went to live as permanent members of the Washington household. John Custis' two older daughters stayed with their mother, Eleanor Calvert Custis, who would later remarry and bear sixteen more children.

Washington delighted in the care of his two grandchildren. Though constantly busy with his personal estate and the affairs of his country, he took the time personally to oversee the education and upbringing of the two young additions to his family. Late in 1785 he began to look for a person who could serve both as his secretary and as a tutor to the children. In one letter to an acquaintance in England he wrote, "I have a little boy something turned of four, and a girl of six years old living with me, for whom I want a Tutor. They are both promising children, the latter is a very fine one." He sent out other inquiries, including one to Noah Webster, and by early February, 1786, he had temporarily hired William Shaw.

Shaw was soon replaced by Tobias Lear, a twenty-four-year-old Harvard graduate who had studied in Europe. Washington's offer to Lear was tempting: "Mr. Lear, or any other who may come into my family in the blended characters of preceptor to the Children, and as a Clerk or private Secretary to me, will sit at my Table, will live as I live, will...be treated in every respect with civility, and proper attention." Lear's acceptance of these bright prospects began a relationship with the family that would last throughout Washington's lifetime.

Recalling her early education, Nelly mentioned not only Tobias Lear but also another tutor, named Gideon Snow, and told of occasions when David Humphreys, Washington's aide, taught her to recite passages from the *Iliad*. Nelly would never attend college; that privilege was reserved for boys. But her loving grandparents saw to it that she had the best education society could offer young women of her time.

Nelly's first opportunity to receive formal classroom training came in 1789 when Washington became President and took his family to live in New York, the first capital of

by Donald Jackson

An oil portrait of Miss Eleanor Parke Custis at the height of her youth and beauty, thought to be painted by the English artist James Sharples while he was working in America between 1793 and 1801
WOODLAWN PLANTATION, MOUNT VERNON, VA.

the new United States. The trip from Mount Vernon was marked by a good deal of ceremonial pomp. When Martha and the children arrived in New York in late May, Martha reported in a letter home that Nelly had complained of feeling a bit sick from the carriage travel and that "dear little Washington" seemed lost in the confusion of crowds and parades along the way.

Once settled in the new capital, Martha turned her thoughts to the children's education. Nelly was privately tutored in music and art, one art teacher being the famed painter, historian, and playwright William Dunlap. Her music instructor was Alexander Reinagle of Little Queen Street, an Englishman who was then writing some of the best music of his century. In addition to these private lessons, Nelly was enrolled with Mrs. Graham of Maiden Lane, a woman who kept a fashionable school for young ladies. Mrs. Graham advertised a curriculum of reading, English, grammar, plainwork, and embroidery, in addition to geography, painting, music, dancing, and French. For at least seven months, Nelly went to the little academy along with the children of several prominent New Yorkers. Then the Washington family left New York for Philadelphia, which had become the second capital of the young nation and was also the cultural center of America.

Nelly was eleven when the Washingtons moved into the Robert Morris house in Philadelphia. Their neighbors were the Morrises—already good friends—who had renovated and occupied the house next door. The Morrises' daughter Maria became the first of Nelly's companions in Philadelphia; their friendship had already been launched the year before when Martha and the children visited the Morris home. Now Maria and Nelly began to gather around them a small circle of young girls who were not to take their friendships lightly and who would continue their correspondence well into their adult years.

Elizabeth Bordley, nearly two years older than Nelly and Maria, soon joined this select circle. Her father was John Beale Bordley, the man Washington had appointed to receive subscriptions to the Bank of the United States. Young Elizabeth Bordley's lifelong friendship with Nelly, and the resulting exchange of letters, is our main source of information about Nelly's life. The circle also included at various times Elizabeth Allen, whose father had served in the Continental Congress, and Susan Randolph.

The life that turned these girls into winsome, chattering teen-agers was the best the nation could provide. Philadelphia was the hub of the world to Nelly; her beloved "Grandpapa" was the President and the idol of his country; Nelly was in love with everyone and everything, and the world seemed eager to return the affection. With some dismay, grandmother Martha wrote home, "I hope when Nelly has a little more gravitie she will be a good girl. At Present—she is I fear half crazy." But Martha loaded up the whole giggling crowd for rides about town in the presidential carriage, and tolerated a parrot named Snipe and a dog named Frish.

Strict attention was paid to Nelly's continuing education. She studied art with Jean Pierre Henri Elouis, and her dancing master was James Robaret. She learned languages also, apparently becoming proficient in Italian, French, and Spanish. In writing to her friends, she delighted in the small vanity of carelessly dropped foreign phrases: *Votre très humble servante,* and *de tout mon coeur.* She taught her

81

parrot to sing "Pauvre Madelon" in French. Washington, obviously proud of his talented granddaughter, continued her musical training and made her play for company.

Nelly once sent a note to Elizabeth Bordley saying she could not come to a party because "we have a large company of the *Honorable Congress* to dine with us, & I must not be so remiss to go out in the evening as they like *to hear musick*." She added, with what was becoming a tendency toward sharp-tongued evaluation of her peers and elders, that the congressmen "do not know one note from another."

Nelly was beginning to notice young men, not always with approval. One hapless lad she labeled a "little milk and water monkey." When she was paid compliments and given adoring verses by Andrew Allen, she was flattered by the attention but was not yet ready to take any boy seriously. Still, she was reaching the age when men were going to find her attractive, a few exceedingly so, and Grandpapa Washington thought it time to offer some counsel on the matter. On the occasion of an important social event in January, 1795, when Nelly was off visiting in Georgetown, Washington wrote one of his few letters to her that have survived. In it, he fondly warned her that her current indifference to men would soon change, and advised her to use her reason as well as her emotions in choosing a husband. (See box on page 84.)

In the fall of 1795, Nelly experienced her first prolonged absence from her grandmother. She went to visit her mother at Hope Park, Virginia, a rather isolated estate twenty miles from Alexandria. Then she went on to Georgetown to visit her older sister Martha, now married to Thomas Peter. Nelly found it hard to part with her grandparents. She wrote to Elizabeth Bordley, "I have gone through the greatest trial, I ever experienced—parting with my beloved Grandmama. This is the first separation

for any time since I was two years old. Since my father's death, she has been even more than a mother to me, & the President most affectionate of Fathers. I love them more than any one."

By May of 1796, Nelly was pleased to write that she would be spending the summer at Mount Vernon with her grandmother. In September she was still at the family estate and told Elizabeth, "I am more & more attached to this place, & in spite of the ague & fever, prefer it to all others." She had been plagued by malaria and her grandmother had suffered four bouts of it, but she loved Mount Vernon anyway. "I ride sometimes on horseback, walk, read, write French, work, play & always think the weeks go off too fast." Although Nelly was to return to Philadelphia for the winter, Washington's second term as President was expiring early in 1797, and in March of that year, the whole Washington family left the capital to return to Mount Vernon permanently. Nelly's baggage was predictably burdensome. Washington good-naturedly complained to Tobias Lear that "On one side I am called upon to remember the Parrott, on the other to remember the dog. For my own part I should not pine much if both were forgot." Though Nelly grieved for her lost friends, she was happy to return to the country. "When I look at this noble river," she wrote to Elizabeth, "& all the beautifull prospects around, I pity all those who are in cities, for surely a country life, is the most rational & most happy of any, and all the refinements of Art and Luxury are nothing in comparison to the Beauties of Nature."

Nelly had absorbed her grandfather's strong interest in horticulture. A flower that she loved especially, and mentioned several times in her letters, was the woodbine, or jessamine, an evergreen with yellow flowers that bloomed in April. She wrote to Elizabeth's father to thank him for

LEFT: *While at Mount Vernon in 1796, Benjamin Latrobe sketched this family scene showing Nelly Custis standing, and Martha Washington seated behind the table.* RIGHT: *Nelly's lifelong friend and confidante, Elizabeth Beale Bordley, painted by Gilbert Stuart in 1797 when she was twenty.*

one of his works on agriculture, saying that with his instruction she hoped to become "a great *Farmer*" in time.

As much as Nelly loved the country life, it was hard for her to stay away from the stimulation of society. After little more than a month at home she went up to Washington for the races, and reported to Elizabeth about a ball at the Union Tavern. She evidently attracted quite a bit of attention by dancing six times with a new acquaintance, Charles Carroll. He was the son of one of the signers of the Declaration of Independence, a wealthy lad whose estate, Homewood, would later become a part of the Johns Hopkins University campus in Baltimore.

Nelly resented the rumors caused by her dancing with young Carroll. "I wish the world would not be so extremely busy, & impertinent," she wrote Elizabeth. "E. P. Custis desires not its notice, & would thank those meddling *reporters* never to mention her name. I wish they would also allow her to *Marry* who she *pleases*, & *when she pleases* without perpetually *engaging her to those she never had a chance of marrying and never wished* to be united [to]."

There was no way for Nelly to enjoy the obscurity she claimed to want. By now she was such a charmer that the world—certainly *her* world—was hopelessly her captive. One visitor to Mount Vernon, Joshua Brookes, detailed her appearance: "She appeared to be about twenty, dressed in white sprig muslin tied around her waist with a sky-blue silk cord with six round balls at the end, head-dress fillet round her head and hair hanging down in ringlets between three turns of the fillet; no powder, about 5ft 4 high, middling stature and size. Silk stockings. Black shoes with large roses. She appeared modest, well-bred, intelligent, and sensible, has a piercing eye, grecian nose, made judicious remarks and conversed with propriety."

The wonderful days raced by. "I never have a dull or

lonesome hour, never find a day too long," Nelly wrote to a Philadelphia friend. She finally got her fill of dancing, however, and confided to Elizabeth in the spring of 1798 that she didn't want to dance again until the next winter: "I almost lamed myself last Winter."

Later in 1798 a new member was added to Washington's household staff. Lawrence Lewis was a nephew of Washington's, a thirty-year-old widower whose wife had died in childbirth seven years earlier. He was, as Nelly would later write, "not the most energetic of men," and of course he was much older than she. ("Connect yourself with a person of congenial age," Washington had advised Nelly's sister a couple of years earlier, "for youth and old age, no more than winter & summer, can be assimilated. . . .") But at a time when she might have chosen any man of wealth and attainment in the nation, Nelly fell in love with Lawrence Lewis.

"Cupid, a small mischievous Urchin, who has been trying sometime to humble my pride, took me by surprise," Nelly wrote to Elizabeth. "When I had abused & defied him, & thought my heart impenetrable, he slyly called in Lawrence Lewis to his aid, & transfixed me with a Dart, before I knew where I was."

The wedding was planned for February 22, 1799, the President's birthday. Because Nelly was still a minor, and Washington not her legal guardian, he went up to Alexandria and arranged a guardianship so that he could consent to the marriage.

There was some controversy over what Grandpapa should wear to the wedding. Nelly wanted to see him resplendent in a handsome new uniform which had been made for him. It was splendidly embroidered and topped by a "magnificent white plume" given to him by an old friend, Major General Charles Cotesworth Pinckney.

ADVICE FROM A
DOTING GRANDFATHER

Dear Nelly:

. . . Let me touch a little now on your Georgetown ball, and happy, thrice happy, for the fair who were assembled on the occasion, that there was a man to spare; for had there been 79 ladies and only 78 gentlemen, there might, in the course of the evening, have been some disorder among the caps . . . notwithstanding the apathy which one of the company entertains for the "*youth*" of the present day, and her determination "never to give herself a moment's uneasiness on account of any of them." A hint here; men and women feel the same inclinations to each other *now* that they always have done, and which they will continue to do until there is a new order of things, and you, as others have done, may find, perhaps, that the passions of your sex are easier raised than allayed. Do not therefore boast too soon or too strongly of your insensibility to, or resistance of, its powers. . . .

When the fire is beginning to kindle, and your heart growing warm, propound these questions to it. Who is this invader? Have I a competent knowledge of him? Is he a man of good character; a man of sense? For, be assured, a sensible woman can never be happy with a fool? What has been his walk in life? Is he a gambler, a spendthrift, or drunkard? Is his fortune sufficient to maintain me in the manner I have been accustomed to live, and my sisters do live, and is he one to whom my friends can have no reasonable objection? . . . Have I sufficient ground to conclude that his affections are engaged by me? Without this, the heart of sensibility will struggle against a passion that is not reciprocated; delicacy, custom, or call it by what epithet you will, having precluded all advances on your part. The declaration, without the *most indirect* invitation of yours, must proceed from the man, to render it permanent and valuable, and nothing short of good sense and an easy unaffected conduct can draw the line between prudery and coquetry. It would be no great departure from truth to say, that it rarely happens otherwise than that a thorough-paced coquette dies in celibacy, as a punishment for her attempts to mislead others, by encouraging looks, words, or actions, given for no other purpose than to draw men on to make overtures that they may be rejected. . . .

Yours affectionately,

George Washington

Washington would have nothing to do with the flashy outfit. He wore his old Continental blue and buff uniform with a cocked hat and plain black riband cockade. But before he packed the new uniform away, he gave Nelly a beautiful plume.

During that summer, Nelly and Lawrence rode off for a honeymoon in the mountains, then made protracted visits to the homes of friends. A house called Woodlawn was being built for them within sight of Mount Vernon, and they remained at the old family estate until the new place was ready for them.

George Washington was now an old man. "My glass is almost run," he liked to say. And on December 12, 1799, he contracted the illness which was to cause his death two days later. Nelly was herself ill from the birth of her first child. Perhaps she knew, as she sobbed and tossed through the days of despair between Washington's death and burial, that nothing could ever again be the same for her. Her one consolation lay bundled warmly in a crib by the fireplace: Frances Parke Lewis.

Washington's death began a chain of events that turned Nelly from a smiling, happy girl into an embittered old woman. By 1804 she had lost two children and the grandmother she loved so much. "I look back with sorrow, & to the future without hope," Nelly wrote to Elizabeth. "It appears to be a dream long passed away, so heavily has time passed to me." For all the love and care that her doting grandparents had lavished on Nelly, they had not provided her with a reserve of inner strength and self-reliance. George and Martha were the bulwark on which she depended; with both of them dead, she could not cope with the real and imagined troubles which beset her.

Her husband proved little consolation for Nelly. Times were hard, and Lawrence seemed not to be a good man-

ager. The Lewises' fortunes dwindled. Nelly's letters conspicuously lacked talk of her feelings for her husband, but their marriage appears not to have been a happy one. In the struggle of living on a diminished income, Nelly quite lost her taste for the dancing that had once excited her, and told her friend Elizabeth that she had given up music and painting for "Pickling, preserving, & *puddings*." "Indeed I am become a very humdrum character." It was worse than that; she had become a bore. She was full of self-pity, indulging in a jittery concern for her children that tended toward paranoia, and apprehensive about her own health. She dosed herself constantly with Seidlitz powders to treat her headaches, and in later years claimed that "Without Seidlitz, I could not live." (The medication was, in fact, only a mild cathartic.)

Many of Nelly's tribulations were real. She was truly plagued by illnesses that became disabling toward the end of her life. She endured the death of seven of her eight children, presiding at the deathbeds of some. When her daughter Agnes contracted a fatal illness while at school in Philadelphia, Nelly hastened to nurse her through the end, and later tortured herself with the speculation that the fifteen-year-old girl might have been sealed alive in her coffin.

Both Nelly's husband and her daughter Angela died in 1839, and Nelly went to live on her son Lorenzo's estate. Called Audley, the farm was located in the Shenandoah Valley, and was even more isolated than Woodlawn. "This beautiful autumn I cannot participate in," Nelly wrote to Elizabeth. "I cannot go out of the house or in a carriage, I stand at the door, & seeing the green wheat, the beautiful mountains, inhale the sweet air, but my limbs are weak & I despair now of ever recovering entirely." That was in 1850. She died in March, 1852, in total ob-

scurity, with no one to attend her but Lorenzo's widow.

Among Nelly's papers at Mount Vernon is an undated scrap intended for Elizabeth, written very late in her life. Her rushing memories had drawn her back to her early teens when she had known young Andrew Allen. He had written her a poem for her fifteenth birthday which she had kept until her marriage. It began with these lines:

> *To thee fair Maid, let love his homage pay*
> *In Humble song on this auspicious day*
> *Nor view the attempt with too severe an eye*
> *Tho' mean the verse, yet still the subject's high.*

"When I was at Morrisville, Andrew passed a day with us," Nelly wrote; and she had paid a return visit to the Allen home called Neshaminy. Andrew had called Maria Morris and Nelly "sister goddesses," and had spoken of the Schuylkill River as Nelly's mirror. Now she was a broken old lady raking through her memories for a bright gem or two.

"How witty and agreeable he was," Nelly mused. "I certainly should have loved him had I not been too happy and gay to be susceptible." Instead she had chosen Lawrence Lewis, who wrote no poems, said nothing witty, and, at least to her mind, was not always agreeable.

One more letter made it plain that Andrew was in Nelly's thoughts. She asked Elizabeth for a likeness of him as he appeared in later life, and then in a single line totaled up the regrets, the unfulfilled years, the misery that had begun when her girlhood ended at Mount Vernon so many decades ago: "Do tell me if he ever spoke of me at all, & what he said."

Donald Jackson is currently the editor of the George Washington Papers at the Alderman Library, University of Virginia.

THE WORLD'S TALLEST BUILDING

by Spencer Klaw

O f the skyscrapers that sprang up in American cities in the early years of this century and embodied in masonry and steel the swaggering vitality of American technology and American business enterprise, none took so firm a grip on the public imagination as the Woolworth Building. From the day that Frank W. Woolworth, the inventor of the five-and-ten-cent store, let it be known that he intended to erect the world's tallest building on a site in lower Manhattan, the newspapers were filled with accounts of its construction and encomiums to its builders. The New York *Sun* compared the building to the Colossus of Rhodes, and described it as the "crowning glory of the builder's art." The *Press* ran a story headed WOOLWORTH BUILDING MARVEL OF THE AGE. In 1912, as work on the 792-foot structure was nearing an end, a *Brooklyn Citizen* reporter, sacrificing journalistic objectivity on the altar of patriotism, wrote that now the whole world would have to acknowledge that "for ingenuity, daring and effectiveness the American architects and engineers are far ahead of the master builders of this or any other age."

To celebrate the completion of the building, Woolworth invited some eight hundred guests to a dinner honoring the architect, Cass Gilbert. The dinner was held on April 24, 1913, in an improvised banquet hall on the twenty-seventh floor of the new building, and the diners included such notables as the artist Charles Dana Gibson, the poet Edwin Markham, steel tycoons Charles Schwab and Elbert Gary, the financier Otto Kahn, the writer Richard Harding Davis, three U.S. senators, seventy-eight congressmen, and the lieutenant governor of Massachusetts. At 7:30 the lights in the room were dimmed, and a Western Union operator flashed a signal to the White House, where President Wilson was waiting to press a button to light up

Like a Gothic relic of the Middle Ages, the tower of the Woolworth Building (left) pierced the skies over Manhattan in the 1920's.

87

In nooks and crannies of the Woolworth Building's interior, twelve bas-relief caricatures of the principals were fashioned with a splendid wit; at left is the building's architect, Cass Gilbert.

"The Cathedral of Commerce," it was called, the "Great Work of the Age," the "Eighth Wonder of the World," and hundreds of thousands—perhaps millions—of tinted postcards were run off to show that world New York's most spectacular symbol. The night scene above probably was produced in 1915.

It is said that Woolworth's own bas-relief caricature (right) caused him to laugh until he wept. He ordered it never to be removed. The old boy was not without a certain ineffable style.
BOTH: DAVE SAGARIN

the whole building with eighty thousand bulbs. "A second later," the New York *American* reported, "waiting thousands in New York and its suburbs saw, flashing out in outlines of fire, the greatest mountain of steel and stone ever erected by man—the gigantic Woolworth Building."

Later, after Woolworth had presented Gilbert with a silver loving cup big enough for a horse to drink from, a poem in Gilbert's honor was read by the poet and essayist William Winter. Winter had retired in 1909 after a long career as the dramatic critic of the New York *Tribune*, where he had been known to his colleagues as Weeping Willie because of the lugubrious elegies he composed to mourn the passing of actors whose work he had admired. The poem he produced on this occasion began dolefully enough, referring to such long-vanished centers of civilization as Babylon and Tyre, and noting that "ravens flit and serpents hiss / O'er what was once Persepolis." But by the time Winter had reached the tenth stanza his poetic tears had dried. New York, he seemed to be saying, might be saved from the fate of Babylon and Tyre by great artists like Cass Gilbert, chosen by destiny "To hail the future and ordain / Triumphant Beauty's perfect reign."

The organization of the banquet—and, presumably, the enlistment of President Wilson's services as an electrician—was the work of a publicity man named Hugh McAtamney. He had been retained by Woolworth on the theory that the Woolworth Building, if properly publicized, would operate as a great magnet, pulling millions of new customers into Woolworth stores all over the United States. Long before the building was finished McAtamney had been planting newspaper stories celebrating the wonders of a country where a man who had started out as a $3.50-a-week store clerk was not only putting up the tallest building the world had ever seen, but was paying its entire cost—$13,500,000—out of his own pocket.

But popular fascination with the building, whose fifty-eighth-floor observation gallery drew more than 300,000 visitors a year during the 1920's, was not simply a product of inspired press-agentry. The Woolworth Building was not only the tallest building in the world, it *proclaimed* its tallness in a way that filled the beholder's breast with awe and wonder. This was not generally true of skyscrapers built before 1913, most of which were actually designed so as to play down their height. A case in point was the Metro-

politan Life Tower, which stood (and still stands) on Madison Square, two miles north of the Woolworth Building. Modeled on the campanile of St. Mark's, in Venice, it was, when it was completed in 1910, the tallest building in the world. But as John Burchard and Albert Bush-Brown complained in *The Architecture of America*, the architect was seemingly unable to top off the structure "without stuttering through successive strata of balconies, cornices, roofs, more cornices, pavilions and spires"—all of which had the effect of seeming to press the building down into the ground. By contrast, the Gothic design of the Woolworth Building featured prominent white piers that soared straight up into the sky for seven hundred feet before terminating in flying buttresses and the lacy filigree of the building's crown.

The building's rich Gothic ornamentation also conveyed the uplifting thought that business enterprise in America was more than just a sordid struggle for material gain. This message made a particularly deep impression on S. Parkes Cadman, D.D., S.T.D., L.H.D., the author of the foreword to an elegantly illustrated booklet about the building that Woolworth arranged to have printed up. Dr. Cadman, a Brooklyn clergyman sometimes identified in the local press simply as "the noted divine," wrote, "When seen at nightfall bathed in electric light as with a garment, or in the lucid air of a summer morning, piercing space like a battlement of the paradise of God which St. John beheld, [the Woolworth Building] inspires feelings too deep even for tears. The writer looked upon it and at once cried out, 'The Cathedral of Commerce' . . . ."

In 1913 Frank Woolworth was sixty-one years old and nearing the peak of a dazzling business career. Born on a farm in upstate New York, he had been seized by the notion, after years of clerking in small general stores, that buyers would flock to an establishment where there would be no haggling over prices; where the merchandise would be spread out so that everyone could inspect it for himself; and where—most important of all—no item would cost more than a dime. In 1879 Woolworth opened the world's first successful five-and-ten-cent store, in Lancaster, Pennsylvania. Soon he had a small chain of such stores, each identified by the distinctive red front that was later to be copied by S. S. Kress, S. H. Kresge, and other competitors. As the chain grew, Woolworth was able to buy goods in larger and larger quantities and at lower and lower prices. This in turn enabled him to offer the public better bargains, thereby assuring the success of the new Woolworth stores that were soon being opened at a rate of twenty or thirty a year. In 1911 Woolworth persuaded the proprietors of four smaller chains to combine their businesses with his; when the merger was consummated he controlled a total of more than six hundred five-and-ten-cent stores in the United States, Canada, and England.

In the lobby of the Woolworth Building, hunched up under an ornate ceiling beam, there is a small sculptured caricature of Woolworth. He is shown nursing an oversize nickel, and it is a fact that in real life Woolworth watched nickels, and even pennies, very carefully. Once, in 1890, just before leaving on a trip to Germany, he sent a circular letter to his executives pointing out that "postage on letters to Bremen is five cents per half ounce so you must use thin paper and envelopes to save expense. . . ." Many years later, when he was making millions of dollars a year, he was not above keeping his confidential secretary and the office porter after hours to help him locate a quarter that had disappeared from his change purse. Like other self-made men, he extolled the virtues of hard work. "Many young men fail because they are not willing to sacrifice," he once wrote. "No one ever built a business on thoughts of having a good time."

But Woolworth saw no point in plain living for people who, like himself, had earned the right to live otherwise. His imposing stomach, customarily draped in a dark vest with white piping, testified to the quantities of food he ate. "He scorned exercise in any form," his biographer, John K. Winkler, writes, "and at all hours of the day and night indulged a fondness for rich foods—lobster, rarebits, etc. He doted upon bananas, a delicacy of which he had been deprived in youth, and preferred them overripe."

Woolworth also liked big houses and costly furnishings. From 1901 until his death in 1919 he lived mainly in a thirty-room mansion situated at Fifth Avenue and Eightieth Street in Manhattan, a home whose second-floor drawing room was equipped with a large organ. Although Woolworth had never managed to learn to play a musical instrument, and had a hard time carrying a tune, he had a passion for music. The organ was a mechanical one, activated, like a player piano, by rolls of perforated paper, and Woolworth liked to entertain friends by sitting at the console and pressing buttons that would throw the room into blackness and then flood it with colored light— now amber, now green, now deep mauve—to match the mood of the music.

Later, with the help of a vice president of the Aeolian-Skinner Organ Company, Woolworth contrived to add pictorial effects to these performances. In Winkler's words, "Just before the opening of a great orchestral classic, with the room in darkness, a magnificent oil portrait of the composer—Wagner or Beethoven, Liszt or Mendelssohn—

would appear in a panel at the top of the wall, at first faintly, then growing clearer and clearer until the vision was enveloped in light. So lifelike was the apparition that the composer himself seemed present, listening to his own music." Still later Woolworth added meteorological effects. By pressing the right button, Winkler writes, he could make lightning flash, thunder crash, and "rain descend—behind the walls—in torrents so realistic as to make guests wonder how they were going to get home without a drenching."

Woolworth liked opulence in his business as well as his personal life, a taste whose indulgence he justified on the ground that it was good public relations. "You have no idea the impression our fine new office makes on visitors," he wrote in a letter to the company's store managers in 1905. "The five and ten cent business is no longer a Cheap John affair." At the time, the company had just moved into new quarters in lower Manhattan, overlooking City Hall Park, where Woolworth worked at a great mahogany-and-gold desk in a richly furnished green-and-gold office that Winkler describes as "a chromatic joy." But impressive as this was, Woolworth was not satisfied. He felt that he and the company must have a building of their own, one which would advertise not just to business visitors, but to the whole world, the wealth and scope of the enterprise he had founded. And so in 1909 he bought land on Broadway, on the west side of City Hall Park, and the following spring he asked Cass Gilbert to design a suitable company headquarters to be erected on this site.

Cass Gilbert was fifty years old in 1910, a tall man, with a lofty forehead, who wore rimless pince-nez and an imposing handlebar moustache. According to the *Dictionary of American Biography*, he was "purposely impressive in manner and rather pompous at times." Gilbert's biographer adds maliciously, "It was said in the Century Club in New York that he could give the most convincing exposition of the obvious that had ever been heard there." As a young man he had served an apprenticeship to Stanford White. Later, in practice for himself—first in St. Paul, Minnesota, and then in New York—he had designed a number of large and important buildings, including the Minnesota State Capitol and the elaborately neoclassical United States Custom House on Battery Park in Manhattan.

Among architects Gilbert was perhaps admired more for his skill in handling big and difficult jobs than for his felicity as a designer. Nevertheless, it was Gilbert's idea of how a skyscraper should look, rather than his reputation for efficiency, that seems to have recommended him to Woolworth. In 1905 Gilbert had completed a twenty-three-story Gothic-styled office building at 90 West Street, just a few minutes' walk from the site where Woolworth planned to build. It was—and is—a building of considerable grace and elegance, conforming to the dictum of the great Chicago architect, Louis H. Sullivan, that a skyscraper should be "a proud and soaring thing." Woolworth knew the building's owner, General Howard Carroll, and it is likely that he settled on Gilbert as his architect because the clean vertical lines and intricate Gothic detail of the West Street building struck him as pretty much what he would like in a building of his own.

From the start of their association, Woolworth severely tested Gilbert's well-established expertise in the handling of clients. While continually urging the architect to get on faster with the job, Woolworth repeatedly held things up by his own indecisiveness. To begin with, he was unable to decide how high a building he wanted. At first he talked of a forty-two-story structure, just tall enough to overtop the Singer Building, which was then the world's second-tallest skyscraper, being exceeded in height only by the Metropolitan Life Tower. But in August, 1910, the two men met in London, and Woolworth said he had decided he could not afford to tie up as much money as would be needed for a forty-two-story building. He asked Gilbert to make plans for a building about twenty-five stories high, to which a tower might be added at a later time.

Within a few weeks the projected building began to grow again. By November, 1910, it had reached, on paper, a height of 620 feet, eight feet higher than the Singer Building. Before another month had passed, with Gilbert's draftsmen hard at work designing the steel framework for a 620-foot building, Woolworth was telling Gilbert that he was not sure that 620 feet was tall enough. By going ninety or a hundred feet higher, he pointed out, they could overtop the Metropolitan Life Tower as well as the Singer Building, and make the Woolworth Building the tallest in the world.

This was fine by Gilbert. The architect had, in fact, egged Woolworth on by having the Metropolitan Life Tower measured, and providing Woolworth with the information that it was exactly seven hundred feet two inches tall. But Gilbert warned his vacillating client that if he wanted a seven-hundred-foot-plus building he would have to decide on it right away, or else incur the considerable cost of modifying the foundations of the building, work on which had already started, to carry the weight of a heavier structure. Even so, Woolworth hesitated for another month. Then, in January, 1911, he formally approved sketch plans for a building that would rise to a height of at least 750 feet, and the draftsmen in Gilbert's office, throwing away the old drawings, began work at once on a new set

Gilbert also had to put up with Woolworth's penny pinching. This took the form, at times, of trying to get people to work for him for nothing, or for a fraction of what they usually were paid. Thus after agonizing for months over the choice of a general contractor, Woolworth told Louis J. Horowitz, president of the Thompson-Starrett Company, one of New York's leading construction firms, that he would like Horowitz to have the job. But he added that he knew another builder who was ready to do the job for

The elegance of the self-made man is given permanent expression in this portrait of Woolworth in the year of his Building—1913.

nothing—for the sake of the prestige, Woolworth said—and that he thought Horowitz should do likewise. ("I had the feeling," Horowitz recalled later, "that Mr. Woolworth was turning on me, as if it were a fire hose, his customary way of buying goods for his five-and-ten-cent stores.") Horowitz continued to insist on a $300,000 fee, and eventually Woolworth signed on his terms.

A month or so later Woolworth tried the same trick on Gilbert, suggesting that other architects just as distinguished as Gilbert would have been happy to take on the Woolworth Building job for a lot less than the five per cent fee that the two men had agreed on earlier. Gilbert, who had been working on plans for the building for nearly a year, was not impressed. "I can only say," he wrote Woolworth, "that if the proposition had been offered to me I would have refused it but that is neither here nor there." In the same letter Gilbert noted that over the past three months his office had "entirely reorganized the plans of your building, working out its great structural, mechanical and engineering problems and its exceptional problems of design, and filing the drawings with the Building Department in just ninety calendar days. If there is any record of structural planning to equal this I am not familiar with it." Gilbert added that he had been impelled to accomplish this feat "in order to progress the building so as to save you the heavy interest charges on the investment and so this office force has been at work night and day and I have paid for the expensive 'overtime' myself."

There was apparently no further talk of Gilbert taking a cut in his fee. Still, as construction got under way Woolworth, who spent many hours each week going over accounts submitted by the contractors, repeatedly called on Gilbert to explain instances of what he considered to be unpardonable waste or extravagance. This was, of course, Woolworth's right, but he exercised it with infuriating diligence. In September, 1911, for example, Gilbert wrote Thompson-Starrett that Woolworth had complained to him about "an item of $2.50 per day for the services of a telephone boy at the building." In a mood, one may guess, of exasperated resignation, Gilbert went on, "It would appear that this is a large price to pay for such services, and I would ask your explanation thereof and in doing so have no doubt that you can place before Mr. Woolworth information that will satisfy him or if some error has been made . . . that you will make correction accordingly." The record contains no hint of what became of the telephone boy.

Even more trying to Gilbert than Woolworth's indecisiveness and his attacks of stinginess was his insistence that he be consulted about matters that most clients would have been delighted to leave to the architect. This was no doubt to be expected of a man who for years had personally picked every item sold in his stores, and who, even when he was running a million-dollar business, would sometimes walk into a store, unannounced, and rearrange the window

THE BUILDING AS A MATTER OF STEEL: *While the ground is broken and prepared on the skyscraper's site at Broadway and Park Place, at the top of this page, painters on a scaffold render a vision of the future on an adjoining wall for the edification and instruction of passersby. At the bottom of this page, the steel skeleton of Woolworth's dream had risen fourteen stories by February, 1912. At the top of the opposite page, the intrepid Charles Duprey, a Brown Brothers photographer, braces himself against wind and vertigo to get a spectacular shot from one of the building's bracketing towers (we wonder if Duprey took a photograph of the equally brave photographer photographing him from the even more lofty height of the central tower). "Topped off" and its upper floors ready for facing, the building is shown, directly right, as it appeared in July, 1912. And at the far right, dangling masons perform some last-minute touch-up work on the structure's intricate façade.*

display. But expected or not, his fussiness about details was aggravating. In February, 1911, for example, Gilbert noted in a memorandum that he had warned Woolworth that "the men in the office were standing around sucking their thumbs, marking time," because of Woolworth's continuing reluctance to commit himself irrevocably to the 750-foot-plus building that he had approved in principle two weeks earlier. At the same time, Gilbert wrote, Woolworth was taking up many hours of his time, and the time of his associates, going "into details of a more or less unmaterial character at this time such as the elevator signal service, mail chutes, bulletin boards, etc., etc." On later occasions he argued with Gilbert about such matters as the proper width of the corridor doors—Gilbert wanted to make them thirty-eight inches wide, but Woolworth thought thirty-six inches was wide enough—and the question of whether or not there should be liquid soap dispensers in the washrooms. He tried hard, though unsuccessfully, to persuade Gilbert to equip the building with steel radiators instead of the cast-iron radiators that Gilbert favored. He personally picked (and then changed his mind about) the transom lifts to be used on the corridor doors, and, shortly before Christmas of 1911, he visited the offices of the Sanitas Manufacturing Company to look over its line of toilets and other bathroom fixtures. Four months later, Gilbert's office records disclose, Woolworth met with one of Gilbert's senior associates and approved the use of Sanitas toilet seats throughout the building. At the same meeting he settled on the design of the levers that would operate the men's room urinals.

Although Gilbert was impelled by professional pride to take strong exception to many of his client's ideas, he seems to have concluded that Woolworth had a perfect right to do whatever he liked with the thirty-foot-square room on the building's twenty-fourth floor that had been reserved for Woolworth's private office. For a long time Woolworth himself was not sure what kind of décor he wanted, but in the summer of 1913, while touring France with his wife and his wife's sister, he had an inspiration. "Stopping one day in Compiègne," his biographer writes, "they visited Napoleon's Palace. Entering the famous Empire Room, it occurred to Woolworth in a flash that here was the answer to the problem. . . . He, too, would have an Empire Room modeled upon Napoleon's, and furnished and decorated even more elaborately."

He began at once to buy suitable antiques and *objets d'art*, and when he got back to New York he called in a decorator to carry out his ideas. In a letter dated February 20, 1914, and addressed to "all stores, United States, Canada and Great Britain," he described the result: "the handsomest office in the country and possibly the world." He went on to give an inventory of its furnishings, reporting that they included wall panels and wainscoting of Vert Campan marble from the north of Italy; a mahogany Empire desk, three feet nine inches by seven feet six

THE BUILDING AS A MATTER OF STYLE:

Designed to refresh and engage the eye with a myriad of details, the Woolworth Building was—and is—a celebration of intricacy. At the left is the ornate Broadway entrance to the building, as shown in a brochure of 1912, and below is the owner's own office; Woolworth sought to outdo Napoleon in his prime, and surely succeeded. Directly right is a modern view of the observation deck, and at the far right, an older shot of the glittering elevators. Below right is one of the entrance arcades, a matter of mosaic and lace and gold leaf; the arcade's soft, indirect lighting lends the whole corridor a mood of fantasy. Or religion. A company brochure maintained that the light "adds to the feeling you have of being in a church."

FALLING STONE ZONE

The owners of the Woolworth Building today are struggling against a potentially desperate problem, one common to many other old skyscrapers: the threat that pieces of the structure will flake off and drop like so many bombs, to the peril of those on the streets below. In March, 1976, for example, a two-story section of bricks sheered off the side of a building on West Thirty-fourth Street in New York and plummetted to the sidewalk. Fortunately, no one was hurt. Not so the luckless pedestrian who paused for a moment at one of Chicago's busiest intersections three years ago; a chunk of falling terra cotta crushed him like an ant. "One could be propelled into a trauma," a New York maintenance contractor remarked in the *New York Times*, "in view of the potential hazards to life and limb."

The problem is both natural and man-made. At the top of a building as high as the Woolworth, for instance, temperatures will vary tremendously within the space of a few hours, alternately swelling and contracting the surface until it is strained quite literally to the breaking point. High winds and the consequent—though minor—swaying involved add their own kinds of pressure. Some buildings may leak, letting the water gather around steel girders; rusting follows and swells until it pops off bricks or slabs of stone and terra-cotta facing. Finally, there is air pollution, an insidious assault that simply eats away at the stone, just as it has in poor, harried Venice.

Altogether, a dismal prospect, and one not easy to correct. One estimate has it that the most minimal repair work on the façades of such buildings runs to about one dollar a square foot—in the case of a structure with as much surface as the Woolworth Building, a matter of several hundred thousand dollars, at least. What to do? Well, until some cheap, practical means of restoration is found, the owners of the Woolworth Building have taken to draping its towers and turrets and gargoyles in huge nets in order to catch falling chunks, as the photograph above illustrates. A temporary and not altogether satisfactory solution, obviously. New Yorkers promenading the vicinity of Broadway and Park Place might reflect, as one contractor did: "We may be running into very dangerous times."

inches; two large round-back armchairs, upholstered in red and pink and gold tapestry, that had been copied from the famous Throne Chair at Fontainebleau; a bronze bust of Napoleon posing as Julius Caesar ("He liked to look as much like Caesar as possible, you know"); and an elaborate mantel clock "reported to have been given to Napoleon by the Emperor of Russia over 100 years ago." The room also contained a large portrait of Napoleon in his coronation robes, copied from a painting at Versailles. After Woolworth's death, in 1919, it was replaced by a portrait of Woolworth himself.

From an engineering standpoint the Woolworth Building presented its designers with no notably difficult or novel challenges. By 1910 builders like Louis Horowitz were thoroughly familiar with steel-frame construction, in which the weight of a building is supported not by its walls but by interior columns of steel. This was how all skyscrapers were built—no one had figured out any other way to erect a very tall building without making its walls impossibly thick at the base—and the Woolworth Building differed structurally from its predecessors mainly in being taller.

With little else to boast about in the way of technological marvels, Hugh McAtamney concentrated on the building's elevators. They were not only the fastest in the world, he informed the press, but they were the first whose position could be determined by a glance at the winking lights on a signal panel, and the first whose movements could be controlled by a dispatcher in telephonic communication with each of his operators.

McAtamney also worked hard to reassure prospective tenants and visitors that they would be protected by every safety device known to elevator science. This was an important fact to emphasize, for elevators at the time were rightly regarded as only a little less dangerous than airplanes. (During the previous three years, the New York *Tribune* reported in 1912, published data indicated that 2,671 Americans had been killed or injured in elevator accidents.) McAtamney pointed out, among other things, that the elevator shafts in the Woolworth Building were constructed so that, if all other safeguards should fail, a plummeting car would act like a giant piston, compressing the air beneath it into a cushion that would bring the car to a gentle stop.

To draw attention to this feature, it was announced that the inventor of the system, a Mr. F. T. Ellithorpe, would personally test its efficacy. Explaining to the New York *Sun* how such a test was usually conducted, Ellithorpe said it was his practice to have the test car hoisted to the top of the shaft by a single heavy rope instead of the usual wire cable. "With a long pole, to which is secured a sharp blade, I am able to reach the suspending rope," he said. "Everything being in readiness, I poke this pole through the top of the cage and saw away at the hempen cable." Displaying a lively gift for narrative, Ellithorpe continued, "Strand by strand it parts faster than I can describe it, and then, with a sound like a muffled pistol shot, the last fibres yield under the tugging load of the car and down the shaft the elevator goes whizzing." As it turned out, Ellithorpe was not in the test car when it whizzed down from the forty-fifth floor of the Woolworth Building to the bottom of the shaft six hundred feet below. In his place were seven thousand pounds of ballast and a glass of water, and McAtamney was able to announce that the air cushion had been so effective that when the car came to rest not a single drop had been spilled.

The esthetic problems that Gilbert was called on to solve were a lot more formidable than the purely technical ones. For more than thirty years, ever since the invention of steel-frame construction and high-speed elevators had made skyscrapers possible, architects had been arguing about how they should look. One faction, centered in New York, thought that skyscrapers, like all large public buildings, should be designed in a classical or Renaissance mode. A rival school, centered in Chicago, whose most eloquent spokesman was Louis Sullivan, considered this esthetically dishonest. Members of this school held that since the skyscraper was a radically different kind of building from any the world had seen before, its form should express that difference. In their view, a properly designed skyscraper should seem to glory in its height. It should impress the beholder with the fact that it was not a pile of stone, like the Washington Monument, but a steel cage enclosed in a tight-fitting skin of glass and masonry. And it should owe nothing to classical, Renaissance, or any other architectural forms of the past.

Gilbert subscribed to all but the last of these propositions. Years later, in explaining why he had chosen Gothic forms and ornamentation for the Woolworth Building, he observed huffily that there had not been time to invent "a new type of architectural detail at all equivalent to that which so beautifully adorns the medieval structures of Europe and which took three hundred years to develop." This ignored the fact that back before the turn of the century Louis Sullivan had been ornamenting the façades of skyscrapers with luxuriant but delicate forms of his own invention—forms that constituted, along with Tiffany glass, America's main contribution to *art nouveau*. But while Gilbert was a resourceful designer, he was not an inspired one, and doubtless he knew better than to try to do what Sullivan had done.

In any case, it is unlikely that Woolworth would have let him make the attempt. Woolworth knew very little about architecture, but he knew what he liked, and what he liked was *old* architecture. As the historian Merle Curti has observed of this era, "The conception of art as a relic of past grandeur and as something to be acquired as an evidence of success and 'culture' dominated the thought of the new men of wealth." At his first meeting with Gilbert, Woolworth produced a photograph of a Victorian Gothic building—although Woolworth did not know what building it was, Gilbert recognized it as the Victoria Tower of the Parliament Building in London—and said that something like that was what he had in mind. This was quite agreeable to Gilbert, who had already shown, with his West Street Building, that by using Gothic forms he could both emphasize the upward thrust of a skyscraper and reveal—or at least indicate—the secrets of its construction.

To be sure, a purely Gothic structure was out of the question. The great architects of the Middle Ages had got their effects in part by using broad areas of windowless wall space, and such areas were ruled out by Woolworth's insistence that windows must run in continuous bands across the building, so that the interior space could be subdivided into large or small offices, with even the smallest offices having adequate light. Furthermore, medieval builders had broken up the planes of their exterior walls with deep recesses and bold projections, a privilege that was denied to Gilbert because its exercise would have cost the building's owner tens of thousands of square feet of rentable floor space.

Architect Cass Gilbert, a man of ponderous dignity, but one capable of translating steel and stone into a thing of much grace

But within these limitations Gilbert gave his client a building as Gothic in spirit as a reasonable man could ask for. Although he went about designing it in a spirit that at times verged on religious exaltation—"The mounting chords of [Verdi's] Stabat Mater kept sounding in my mind while I was piling up that building," he recalled later—he testily denied that he had set out to build a secular cathedral. In the early stages of the building's design, he wrote, he had studied such medieval masterworks as Brussels' City Hall, and the great Cloth Hall at Ypres, and his aim had been to "express the idea of a *civic* or *commercial* building rather than of an ecclesiastical one." He went on to suggest, without naming names, that people like the "noted divine," Dr. Cadman, might have been well advised to leave architectural criticism to people who knew what they were talking about.

Most architectural critics, while recognizing that the Woolworth Building was not a cathedral, agreed with Dr. Cadman that it was a masterpiece. Montgomery Schuyler, perhaps the most widely read critic of the day, was nearly as effusive in his praise as the Brooklyn minister. "How it cleaves the empyrean and makes the welkin ring as it glitters in the sunshine of high noon," he wrote. "How impressively it looms above its fellows in spectral vagueness, in the gray of the dawn or the haze of twilight."

Good sense and the passage of time require some tempering of Schuyler's praise. The Woolworth Building's tapering crown, guarded by its four satellite pinnacles, looks a bit stiff and awkward, and Gilbert's Gothic façade lacks the serenity of the very best skyscrapers. Compared with the best of Sullivan's work, such as the beautiful miniature skyscraper he built on Manhattan's Bleecker Street in 1897, with its marvelous frieze of *art nouveau* angels, the Woolworth Building seems a little fussy.

But its faults are minor. Surrounded by boring steel-and-glass boxes, the mechanical products of modern architects working routinely in the International Style, the Woolworth Building still has the power to amaze and delight. The bands of Gothic ornamentation that mark the base of the tower, and each of its setbacks, refresh the eye, but do not interrupt its journey as it is drawn upward by the great piers that both conceal and display the building's steel skeleton. On entering the lobby the visitor is instantly infected with the fever of Woolworth's uninhibited and childlike love of the magnificent. The walls are of golden marble from the Isle of Skyros. The high, vaulted Persian ceiling is a glittering green and gold and blue mosaic of stylized flower patterns and exotic birds. To the rear, a noble marble stairway leads up to a branch office of the Irving Trust Company, whose predecessor, the Irving National Bank, once had its headquarters there. High up on the walls, seeming to hold up the ends of the richly ornamented crossbeams, are sculptured figures of Woolworth and some of the people associated with him in the building's planning and construction. They include Cass Gilbert, who is shown holding in his arms, and gravely contemplating through opaque pince-nez, a huge model of the Woolworth Building; Gunvald Aus, the building's structural engineer, who is shown measuring a girder; and Lewis E. Pierson, president of the Irving Bank, who is shown reading the tape coming out of a stock ticker.

A recent historian of the Woolworth Building, Robert A. Jones, suggests that these playful caricatures "belie the ostensible dignity of the setting." He adds, "The whole resplendent display suggests that, at heart, the artists—in behalf of their client—were teasing mammon." But the teasing was clearly affectionate. In Gilbert's view, and in the view of his chief designer, Thomas Johnson, who was responsible for the caricatures, there was nothing wrong—indeed, there was everything right—with a man who wanted to celebrate so exuberantly his own triumphant career as a merchant. And as Jones further points out, it was what the Woolworth Building represented, more than what it was in itself, that fascinated people. A perfect expression of the spirit of America in the 1920's, the great structure symbolized for hundreds of millions of people all over the world, most of whom had seen it only as portrayed in magazines or on postcards, the wealth, the power, and, above all, the exhilarating promise of a country where a poor farm boy like Frank Woolworth could become as rich as Cröesus.

In 1929, when the Chrysler Building was completed, the Woolworth Building lost the title it had held for sixteen years, and today it ranks only eighteenth in height among the skyscrapers of the world. But none of the newer and taller American skyscrapers, built in a time when the world is no longer so entranced by the vigor and the romance of American business enterprise, has generated quite the same excitement. A glimpse of the Empire State Building, however astonishing, does not induce reactions of the kind recorded in *The Spectator* in 1925 by the British biologist and essayist Julian S. Huxley. "Who can forget," he wrote, "the Woolworth Tower (that monument reared on dimes and nickels), as seen from the river as the liner passes, or when it pulls the eye up to incredible heights as you emerge from the subway at City Hall? It is like a cross between a cathedral and one of Mad King Ludwig's palaces, manured to fantastic heights by the glorious megalomaniac spirit of New York. . . . What matter if ecclesiastical Tudor Gothic, richly gilt, seems out of place in an office-building? It *is* a fairy story come gigantically and triumphantly to life, and can never be forgotten."

Spencer Klaw lives, writes, and teaches in New York and is the author of The Great American Medicine Show, *among other books. He wishes to acknowledge his debt in this article to Robert A. Jones for "Mr. Woolworth's Tower: The Skyscraper as Popular Icon," published in the* Journal of Popular Culture *in 1973.*

Subdued and surrounded, the Woolworth Building today is dwarfed by the towering twin monoliths of the World Trade Center.
EMMA LANDAU

LADY-FINGERS

The place, Bedloe's Island in New York Harbor; the time, probably the fall or winter of 1885; the people, unknown (though we can guess that the young man on the left is *not* the Phillip Morris bellhop); the occasion, nothing much—just sitting around on the Statue of Liberty's fingers and toes. The little island had been the scene of considerable carnage for months, as pieces of the lady who soon would lift her torch "beside the golden door" were strewn about like the wreckage from some terrible accident. The triumphant creation of French sculptor Frédéric Auguste Bartholdi, the statue had been presented to the United States, its sections broken down, numbered, and packed into eighty-five huge crates, and the crates loaded aboard the French warship *Isère* and sent to New York, where they arrived on May 17, 1885. A small railroad was built on Bedloe's Island to move things around and about (its tracks can be seen in the background of the picture), a monstrous concrete pedestal was constructed to hold the statue, and on October 28, 1886, the reassembled arms, legs, feet, face, and fingers of perhaps America's most enduring symbol were unveiled. Today, only a certifiable madman would attempt to sit on the lady's fingers.

*　*　*　*　*

This picture was sent to us by Leon Bodycott of Bradenton, Florida, and we continue to invite our readers to send us unusual, dramatic, or "what's going on here?" photographs that they might own. Such photographs should be at least thirty years old, sharp and clear, and have some interesting story connected with them.

As we cannot be responsible for original material, we request that a copy be sent at first. Under no circumstances should glass negatives be mailed. Pictures can be returned only if accompanied by a stamped, self-addressed envelope. AMERICAN HERITAGE will pay $50.00 for each one used.

AMERICAN WOMEN

by Eugene T. Maleska

ACROSS

1 Phillipine machete
5 Full
10 Actress Menken of 19th c. fame
14 Julia —— Grant, a First Lady
18 Shah's land
19 Self-assurance
20 Roofing man
22 "Jacta est ——!"
23 The Lone Eagle's bride
25 —— Lawrence, U.S. ski star
27 Annapolis and Alexandria
28 Writer Joyce Carol
30 Job suffered many
31 Whit or tittle
32 —— -de-lis
33 Eve or Elizabeth
34 Joan, the comedienne
37 Try to get
38 Sportswoman Sears of Boston
41 Pathologist Hamilton
42 Blind and deaf Radcliffe alumna
44 Disencumber
45 Like some Nellies
46 "The ——," magazine first edited by Margaret Fuller
47 Map abbreviations
48 Alfred Steinberg's book about 15-Down
49 Grammar abbreviation
50 Hatchet-wielding Prohibitionist
54 Viscid; cloying
55 —— Huerta, fearless fighter for farm workers
57 Non-citizen
58 Courage
59 Rolling stone
60 Smokers
61 Elementary particles
62 Progenitors
63 Holy, at Lourdes
64 Holdings; estates
66 Kay or Belle
67 American saint
69 Department on the French Riviera
71 "Battle Hymn . . ." writer
72 Copperfield's first wife
73 Town near Judah
74 Grouper of warm seas
75 One, in Rome
76 Contemporary writer and film maker
80 Fiestas
81 Type of verse
83 Skyscraper item
84 Graham or Washington
85 Day or Duke
86 Rousseau hero
87 Soprano Grist of the Met

88 "Every man can rule —— save he that hath her": Hazlitt
90 Items broken by Wilma Rudolph
91 American actress,

95 Stage star with John Drew
97 Explorer-photographer-author from Kansas

born in Tokyo

99 Shield border
100 Swift brute
101 "—— is an island": Donne
102 Poppaea Sabina's spouse

103 Potter's oven
104 Nobel-prize novelist
105 "The Liner —— Lady": Kipling poem
106 Historic periods

DOWN

1 What Mary McLeod Bethune fought
2 Writer Sarah —— Jewett
3 Cantrell or Turner
4 Like Ederle's suit
5 Zaharias' forte
6 Corporeal channel
7 French shooting matches
8 Inner: Prefix
9 Elsie ——, first "interior decorator"
10 Westernizer of Turkey
11 Patron of Elaine's
12 City officials: Abbr.
13 Feminine pronoun
14 Molokai priest
15 Famed First Lady
16 Actress who overcame disease
17 Urchins
21 Slightly damaged

pieces of paper
24 Pulitzer-prize poet
26 Fervency; zeal
29 Mind-boggling time
32 Lack of good sense
33 Gracie of radio fame
34 She wrote "The Fountainhead"
35 Homeric epic
36 Broker-muckraker who ran for President of U.S. in 1872
37 High, low, and reverse
38 Singer John
39 Stair part
40 "Not —— eye in the house"
42 Personnel person
43 Hurons' kin
46 Bells the cat
48 First permanent tooth
50 Magazine spot for

Monroe
51 "Of course," in jive parlance
52 Point on the nose
53 Princeton symbol
54 Canal Zone dam
56 Late-show villain
58 Poison
60 McPherson's foe
61 Put a label on
62 Abolitionist-suffragette Lucy ——
63 Marsh birds
64 Morning hour
65 Conductor Caldwell
66 Synagogue
67 "Grandma" of the art world
68 Caterpillar hairs
70 Painter Bonheur
72 Fighter for women's rights in the Northwest
74 First name of

24-Down
76 Follower of "yes" or "no"
77 She became a Windsor
78 Off-Broadway award
79 Harriet and Ozzie
80 Dam for catching fish
82 Betsy ——, Met soprano
84 "Three —— Horse"
86 De Valera of Eire
87 "Cookie" of baseball
88 Berserk in Burma
89 Gown for Indira
90 S. A. weaverbird
91 Ida Tarbell gained —— as a muckraker
92 Elbe tributary
93 Ballerina Kaye
94 Biblical patriarch
96 Filly's mother
98 Soothing command to a horse

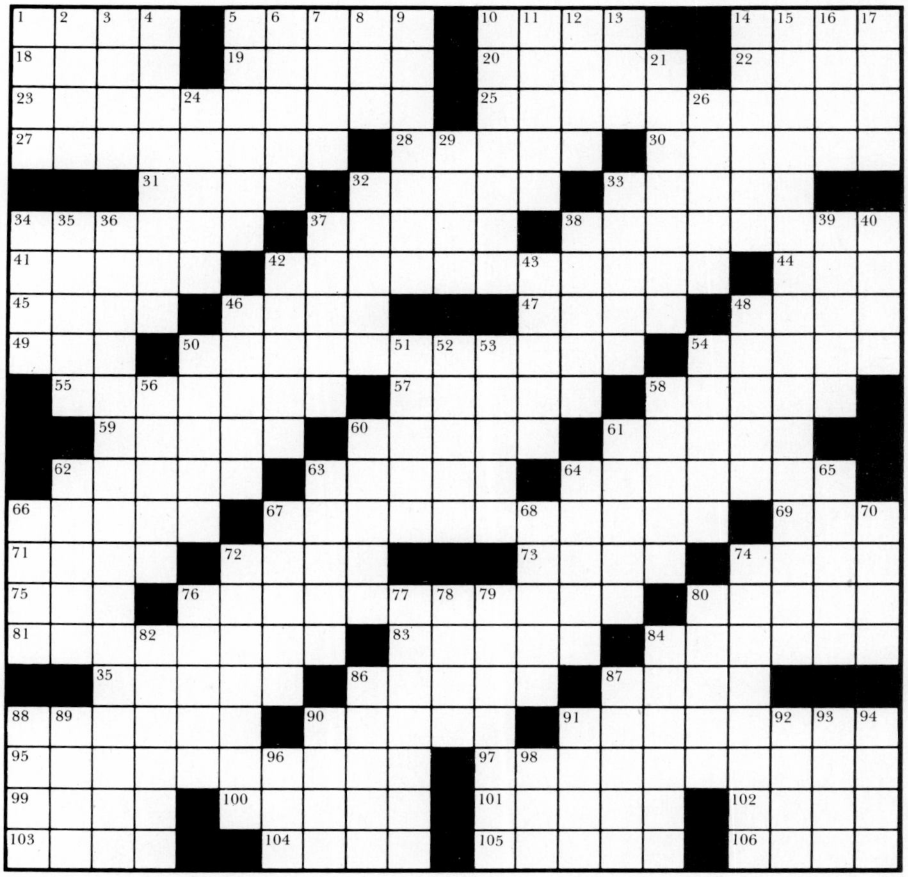

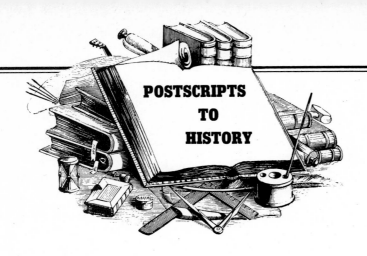

POSTSCRIPTS
TO
HISTORY

DR. RUSH HOLDS FORTH

An unusual follow-up to the article on Benjamin Rush in our December, 1975, issue came to us from Gene DeGruson, curator of special collections at Kansas State College:

"I have in my personal collection the manuscript lectures of Dr. Benjamin Rush, delivered before the College of Philadelphia from November 1, 1790, to February 1, 1791. They were taken down by Elihu Hubbard Smith, a Connecticut wit, physician, poet, and naturalist, and have never been published. Unlike Dr. Rush's published lectures, these are conversational in tone, filled with charming anecdotes and fascinating asides."

Here, then, is Dr. Rush, speaking with cranky, eclectic complacency on love and other serious medical problems:

ON LOVE

"It is the Excess, alone of this passion, which constitutes disease.

"The Symptoms are a perpetual silence concerning, or a constant talking of the person beloved: a love of solitude, especially by moonlight, &c.

"Love, when it is successful, polishes Men, but makes Women appear awkward.

CHARLESTON GETS RID
OF SOME DUMB OLD STUFF

It is, of course, difficult to save old bridges, but there seems little excuse for the feckless hoopla surrounding the recent destruction of a sixty-year-old, seven-hundred-foot bow-string truss that spanned the Kanawha River in Charleston, West Virginia. The *Daily Mail*, a local newspaper, sponsored a contest in which the winner was able to detonate high explosive charges placed along the doomed bridge. Spectators lined the banks of the river, a high school band played, and, the *Mail* exulted, "with a push of a button, the flick of a lever, and a laugh" the winner blew the bridge into eternity (above).

"It is a fact worth remarking that after the Passion is completely formed, the Lover, how much soever he should wish it, can never dream of his Mistress.

"Love affects both Sexes & all Ages.

"The late Gen[l]. Lee told me that when in a certain Village in Germany, he enquired of the Landlord what were the curiosities of the place. The Landlord told him that he had a neighbor who was an hundred & twelve years old. The Gen[l]. desirous to see him, went to the house. On coming to the door he found a very old Man sitting on the sill. 'How do you do?' says the Gen[l]. After this salutation . . . he asked him his age. 'I am,' replied the Old Man, 'Eighty years old.' 'Eighty!' exclaimed the Gen[l].—'I expected to hear you say you were an hundred & twelve.' 'No—' returned the man— 'that is my father.' 'And where is he?' 'He is gone abroad: & I don't much care if he never returns—for,' added the Old Man, bursting into tears—'he last week prevented my marrying a fine young girl and married her himself.'

"The Remote Causes [of love] are Idleness & the reading of Novels & Romances.

"The Proximate Cause is Too much Action in the Brain & Vessels of the Heart.

"Unsuccessful Love, where there is much sighing, fever, &c., is cured . . . by bleeding & blistering.

". . . if this fails . . . the Lover should busy himself in looking out the defects of his mistress, in learning them by rote, & exposing her wherever he can."

ON GOVERNMENT AND DISEASE

"In the simple ages of mankind, stimuli act chiefly on the arterial system; hence fever is produced. With the progress of Civilization, stimuli leave the arterial for the nervous system. . . .

"Sudden Grief, in a Peasant, will produce Fever. In the Second Rank, Melancholly. In the Highest, Syncope or sudden Death. . . .

"This progression of diseases serves not only to distinguish ranks in Society, but to mark the character of Nations. From the records of the Jews, we find that diseases had kept pace with their Moral & Political iniquity, so that they were ripe for that dreadful destruction imposed upon them by Jehovah. . . .

"We have now obtained a new Government. The minds of the people acquire daily new serenity. And if these things can be banished under the operation of our new Constitution, I will venture to predict that nervous diseases will disappear & fevers become, once more, the natural outlet of life."

ON HYPOCHONDRIA

"I once heard of a patient who tho't that he was dead. His Physicians laughing at him, he angrily dismissed them. He was cured by another Physician, who, humoring him and pretending to believe he was dead, proposed opening him. This proposal agitated the dead man so much that he recovered. Yet he always believed that he had been dead and that his physician had restored him to life by his great skill."

DIVISION OF MUSEUM SERVICES, NATIONAL PARK SERVICE, HARPERS FERRY, W.VA.

Conservator Ralph Sheetz restores a chair formerly owned by Nathaniel Hawthorne.

THE RESTORATION FACTORY

Each year a million tourists visit Harpers Ferry, West Virginia, but the building there that contains the greatest collection of historic memorabilia is closed to them. It is a sometime high school that now houses the Division of Museum Services, and it is packed with artifacts from national parks throughout the country, all either awaiting or undergoing restoration to their original condition.

The division was established in 1972 to cope with the great number of National Park Service belongings that were falling prey to age or vandalism. To this repository came clocks, oil paintings, guns, tableware, carriages, and even two tents used by George Washington. (These last needed cleaning, an immense task that required the construction of a tank holding four hundred and eighty gallons of water.)

Six thousand items arrive every year, many of no great merit. As an example, Walter J. Nitkiewicz, the paintings restorer, singled out a drab canvas which had hung in a Puerto Rican fort. "Somebody's accepted it," he said, "and now it will take an Act of Congress to get rid of it."

But every item, however humble, is given painstaking attention and, with the small staff—seven paid "conservators" and a few volunteers—the backlog is growing. Arthur C. Allen, the division's chief, said, "We figure that in about two million years we'll catch up."

MEMENTO MORI

Among the bayonets, pipe bowls, buttons, and other familiar mementos of the American Revolution which were recently on display was one real stunner—the knucklebone from Major John André's big toe.

The grisly relic is owned by Ethel Gove of Northvale, New Jersey. "It's a small, dried up thing," she said. "I never touch it, because I'm afraid it will crumble in my hands." Miss Gove keeps the toe in a bank vault but, in honor of the Bicentennial, she put it on exhibition in the Closter. New Jersey, public library.

In 1820 André's body was exhumed from the grave at the place of his ex-

ecution in Tappan, New York, to be sent back to England. David Doremus, an ancestor of Miss Gove's, served as apprentice to the carpenter hired to build a new coffin for the occasion. Doremus got hold of the piece of bone, built a small wooden reliquary for it, and passed it down to posterity.

Ann Luxner, Director of the Closter Library, doubtfully studies John André's toe bone.

BICENTENNIAL CASUALTY

A year ago, while the nation was gearing up for its Bicentennial festivities, the New York State Department of Education quietly abolished the State Office of History. The office, which formerly had a staff of twenty-eight and a budget of $500,000 a year, was eliminated as part of an economy move by the Department of Education. Five jobs were scrapped, and all other History Office personnel were transferred to other units.

The termination of the office seems a rather paradoxical celebration of the nation's Bicentennial year; most of the money which the Education Department hoped to save was spent by the State Bicentennial Commission. Dr. Louis Tucker, former State Historian and head of the Office of History, commented on the incongruity of cutbacks in both history teaching and in offices such as his own:

"This may be the period in American history when our leaders and those concerned with public policy have the greatest need for a more accurate picture of our history and how our country came into being. I wonder if the Americans who are currently in the White House have read Madison's note on the Constitution, or the Federalist Papers. Until people come to understand how our system was put together, they will have difficulty in directing our country. . . ."

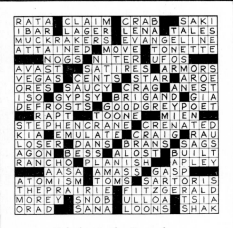

Solution to the December
Crossword Puzzle

WOE TO THE ORANGEMEN—AND TO THE COLOR-BLIND

With St. Patrick's Day approaching, we should mention a strange, little-known monument to Irish contentiousness in Syracuse, New York. It is a traffic light—perhaps the only one of its kind in America—that has the green light on top of the red.

According to John C. McGuire, the unofficial historian of the "Tipperary Hill" area in the western part of the city, the traffic light was first erected in 1925. Dinty Gilmartin, who owned a store nearby, was instantly alarmed and grabbed his telephone: "They got it all mixed up," he told the local boss, John "Huckle" Ryan. "The red is on top; you better get here before something happens."

Sure enough, by the time Ryan arrived, the light was smashed. State law said the red had to be on top, and a new light was put up despite Ryan's protests. It was immediately wrecked, as was the next one. At last the city surrendered, and Tipperary Hill got its upside-down traffic light. It has remained undisturbed ever since.